HOW TO

BE A

gentle

WOMAN

An Hachette UK Company
www.hachette.co.uk

First published in Great Britain in 2019 by Cassell,
an imprint of Octopus Publishing Group Ltd
Carmelite House
50 Victoria Embankment
London EC4Y 0DZ
www.octopusbooks.co.uk

Distributed in the US by
Hachette Book Group
1290 Avenue of the Americas
4th and 5th Floors
New York, NY 10104

Distributed in Canada by
Canadian Manda Group
664 Annette St.
Toronto, Ontario
Canada M6S 2C8

ISBN 978-1-78840-143-2

A CIP catalogue record for this book is available from the British
Library.

Printed and bound in the UK

10 9 8 7 6 5 4 3 2 1

Senior Commissioning Editor: Romilly Morgan
Senior Editor: Pollyanna Poulter
Designer: Jack Storey
Production Controller: Grace O'Byrne
Copy Editor: Alison Tulett
Proofreader: Rachel Cross
Indexer: MFE Editorial
Typesetter: Jeremy Tilston
Illustration, page 6: Alexandria Coe

LOTTE JEFFS

HOW TO

BE A *gentle* WOMAN

THE ART OF SOFT POWER IN HARD TIMES

For Billie

CONTENTS

Gentlewoman
[noun]

A woman who meets the harsh pressures of modern life with thoughtfulness, care and kindness. She is confident; and without needing to shout, exudes a powerful presence.

Introduction

I am rooted, but I flow.
Virginia Woolf [1]

What does the word 'gentle' make you think of?

Seductive whispering?

Weak handshakes?

A bit of a pushover?

As adjectives go, it isn't one we find ourselves typing into our Tinder profiles very often. Gentle sounds old-fashioned. It hasn't really found its place in today's world. Unless it's applied to men of course, because everyone likes a gentleman. Blokes think he's a decent bloke. Straight women think he's a catch – he is refined, confident, kind and solicitous. What is the female equivalent? Lovely lady feels too Jane Austen. Good woman sounds biblical. Cool girl is fine when you're a teenager, but then what?

I believe we need the term gentlewoman now more than ever.

But, in order to define what a 'gentlewoman' is, we need to understand what it means to be 'gentle' as a woman in the modern world.

I believe there is soft power in meeting the pressures of life with a measured, tender, kind approach and this book will help such an attitude infiltrate the way you understand yourself as well as how you choose to live.

Make no mistake, being 'gentle' does not make you weak. A gentlewoman is strong, ambitious, confident, fearless and is always seeking to educate herself. She's living the rough reality but she's doing it with grace. If a gentlewoman smashes a glass ceiling at work, she's sure to pick up all the shards, clearing the way for those coming up behind her.

The idea of a gentlewoman, in the mid-19th century, made its way into popular consciousness via a book called *The English Gentlewoman* [2]. This was a guide for young women of a certain class who were about to 'come out' in society as debutantes, and basically contained all the advice they'd need to lock down a husband. The book's aim was to promote the manners, charm and intellect of an accomplished young woman and it includes etiquette tips and advice about how to ensure that one doesn't come across as too 'learned', because heaven forbid you might know more about something than a man! The book is, unsurprisingly given that it was first published in 1845, not for the modern woman. But the spirit of self-improvement still flourishes within its husband-finding fixation.

From the preface:

The object of the writer is, by the experience of a life passed in those circles which constitute what is called 'the world', to supply those who are entering into a new and busy sphere with some of the practical benefits of observation and reflection; to propound the elements of that species of knowledge, which, contrary to other sciences, is usually acquired by blunders and errors; the lessons of which are often received with mortification, and remembered often with regret.

Reading through this old edition in the British Library made me think that if we put the same amount of considered work into ourselves as these 'Hints to Young Ladies on their Entrance into Society' encouraged, but rather than doing so to become a perfect vision of contrived femininity in order to honey-trap a suitor we did the work for *ourselves*, maybe we'd be on to a new form of female power. A power that we find within and then project outwards, so that we can be happily engaged in the world around us and the people we share it with.

I've been working on my own version of self-improvement over the past decade. After hitting my lowest ebb – dealing with death, family dramas and my own unfulfilling relationship – I found a way to slowly build myself up again. Really getting to know and like myself, finally feeling grounded, confident and happy, and seeing my emotional and physical well-being not in isolation but as intrinsically connected to the other people in my life and the choices I make, became a project I was reaping the benefits of. I learned that it is through care, thoughtfulness and empathy that we truly inhabit our best self rather than just 'activating' it when we think people are watching. And now I feel able to give this way of being a name: it's *becoming* a gentlewoman, and I am on a mission to reframe 'gentle' as a source of soft power in the 21st century.

Soft power

American political scientist Joseph Nye is credited with first defining soft power[3]. The term is most often used in a political sense to mean 'a persuasive approach to international relations, typically involving the use of economic or cultural influence'. But in the context of an individual, demonstrating soft power means:

- Showing rather than telling;
- Connecting with others;
- Listening;
- Taking time to think before acting;
- Playing the long game, not looking for a quick fix;
- Showing empathy and kindness;
- Being diplomatic;
- Building trust.

Most of us already embody some characteristics of a gentlewoman, but the stress of a high-pressure job, a busy social life and demanding relationships with friends, lovers or family can throw us off our course. The result is that we are less kind to ourselves and others, less happy and less able to fulfil our true potential. We react irrationally, make bad decisions and live with a simmering dissatisfaction with the world, which makes us reach for various panaceas: we disappear into social media where we can curate a version of our life and opinions, instead of engaging with the messiness of reality; we drink too much, eat too much, go to the gym too much as we try to appease that sense that something is missing.

Does this feeling that you can't quite settle within yourself resonate? You start projects but abandon them or they just fizzle out before you've achieved anything? You download apps to track your sleep, your workouts or the number of steps you take in a day in the hope that these stats, a solid number you've achieved, will somehow fill the 'lack' in your life of anything more substantially satisfying? I believe this vacuum is the result of living in a world in which, as the philosopher Jean Baudrillard famously wrote: 'The image is more real than the real.'[4]

So much now is surface and while I'm not saying the external signifiers of a good life don't matter – I like a curated Instagram account as much as the next person – I understand it is *simply* aesthetic. Decoration is the last thing you do to something built from scratch. First you must work on the foundations, the structure; construct something strong that will last. If this is how you approach creating the life you want for yourself then everything else enriches rather than comprises your sense of self.

This book will get under the skin of every aspect of your life, from the importance of creating a happy home and delineating a space that is just yours within it, to learning to enjoy being alone. I'll explain how to thrive at work by allowing yourself to be truly seen, and the importance of building meaningful relationships. I'll cover how a gentlewoman knows when to leave a party, has the right clothes for every occasion, always lays the table and makes her bed, is a generous host, is never late or too early, sends handwritten notes, and knows how to use a power drill. These things may seem like frippery to the ungentlewomanly eye, but they matter. They show a respect for yourself and if you care about the little things it stands to reason that you navigate the bigger, more challenging, areas of life with care and attentiveness too.

How to be a Gentlewoman is not a quick-fix ideology. It involves recognizing that the key to better living and greater happiness at work, in love and with our friends and family is something we achieve by looking inwards and then projecting outwards.

Today's gentlewoman is a woman of character. She has a strength born of experience and a charm that lights up a room. She is courteous, even when such a value feels out of step with the JUST DO YOU world in which it is permissible, even encouraged, to operate entirely from a place of self-interest, verging on narcissism. We've started 'celebrating' individuality to the extent that we forget to invite anyone else to our celebration, or show up at theirs. Cherishing what makes you different and unique, enjoying your confidence and cultivating a deep knowledge of, and love for, yourself shouldn't make you self-obsessed. But if it has, this is the wake-up call you need.

When Melania Trump wore a jacket emblazoned with the slogan 'I really don't care, do u?' in the summer of 2018, it represented a nadir of solipsism that although we may not think we are guilty of – we retweet support for good causes, go on marches and never use plastic straws – we often are. How much do we really care about other people's feelings and our own impact on the world around us?

When did you last stop to think about why your work colleague is being extra panicky about a presentation? Or what the barista was thinking while you were talking on your mobile rather than engaging with them at the counter? Or how your mum feels when you don't text her back for a week? Or what's going through your partner's mind each time you forget to ask how their day was before launching into a diatribe about your own?

How often do you see yourself from anyone else's point of view?

BEING A GENTLEWOMAN INVOLVES LEARNING TO PAY ATTENTION TO THE WORLD AROUND YOU

I don't mean a digital detox, that's too much of a short-term solution, which involves escaping from, rather than sensibly dealing with, reality. Just look up once in a while, take out your headphones, turn off push notifications. If you consciously side-step instant gratification for something more meaningfully gratifying you will notice people and their moods, places and their beauty, and you'll notice something new about yourself in the process. Start asking questions, listening to and being interested in people. We need to seek out real-life connections not double taps and follows, allowing ourselves time and space to be empathetic and emotionally astute in our understanding of others...and otherness. Being a gentlewoman today has nothing to do with social class, background, money or professional standing. It has everything to do with a woman knowing herself deeply and using her stability to inspire, lift up or support the people around her.

This book is about cross-examining our default settings, asking why we live and behave the way we do, and if, indeed, we can cut a new path. It will explore the happiness that comes from showing up fully and authentically in every facet of your life. But I know you won't start as a blank slate; if anything you're a piece of stone, weathered somewhat (no offence) and maybe broken in parts with pieces missing, but by the end of this book, I hope you'll have carved out a shape for yourself that is solid and grounded and quite unshakeable.

BUT WHY THIS, AND WHY NOW?

Well, women today are under unbelievable pressure to be everything to everyone: cool, smart, fit, thin (but not too thin!), funny but not mean; a supportive friend, partner and family member; to be successful and liked at work, and to have opinions about politics, art and literature as well as reality TV and Kanye West's latest tweets. It's exhausting. The last thing we need is another book that proposes a quick-fix way of being, another suit of armour – something we can take off and put on in order to become a more appealing person.

In this frantic world, self-improvement 'methods' can feel like further pressure, and finding happiness becomes the next box to tick on our overflowing to-do list. Think how often you reply to the question 'how are you?', with 'busy'.

We wear busyness like a badge of honour. The more tasks we have to do, the more important we feel. But a gentlewoman doesn't need to be busy to feel valued. Of course, there are things you must do, but then there are things you agreed to do when you didn't need to and for the wrong reasons. Maybe you felt guilty that you hadn't spent enough time with your extended family so you agreed to host a big lunch when all you really wanted to do was collapse after a hectic week. Or maybe at work, you say yes to helping out on someone else's project, or being the one who puts the majority of effort in for a presentation – why? Because you think it'll make you look good? Or because you think it's good to be 'insanely busy'? When did being busy equate to being successful?

Busy women are in a constant state of reaction, taking on the next thing and the next thing, but never really engaging properly with anyone or anything – least of all themselves. If you are always responding to what is happening to you, there's less time to be proactive and really think about what *you* want to achieve and how you're going to do it.

A gentlewoman doesn't care about clearing her inbox before filling her outbox. If she did she'd be so exhausted by responding to other people there would be little energy left for her own projects and purposes. It's not pleasant to be around someone who is stressed. Learning to put yourself on top of your to-do list and reframing busyness so that it feels enriching rather than depleting will help you focus on your own flow in life, so you are less susceptible to absorbing other people's franticness.

This book will help you manage stress through kindness – to yourself first, and then, by default, to those around you. We'll learn to recognize when being busy is a positive sign that we are living a full life, and when it means we are piling more and more stuff into our world to fill a void.

Devoting energy to one part of your life doesn't ever need to be at the expense of another. Keeping everything on a slow steady heat, without having to turn one burner off to crank another up to full blast, is a constant effort, but it's worth it.

GET READY TO INTERROGATE HOW YOU LIVE...

I mean *really* live and in the process discover what lies beneath the emotional paraphernalia of work, love, friends and family that comprise the complicated miscellany of modern life. Delving this deep into yourself to find what anchors you isn't easy. It means being vulnerable. And you must be brave to choose gentleness in response to harshness. You may have to unlearn instinctual habits, particularly in your relationships or career, that come from a place of defensiveness, and soften your sharp edges. In an often cut-throat world, it's a challenge to channel negative emotions into gentleness.

You may have to shut out the expectations of your friends and family, online opinions and Instagram-approved aspirations, as well as voices in the media that encourage you to embody predefined tropes. Are you a Mumpreneur, a Slashie, a Xennial, a Snowflake? 'Choose which box you fit into before they fill up,' society seems to scream from behind your phone screen. Labels are designed to contain you, make you easy to understand or 'place' in today's world. But conforming for the sake of fitting a persona is futile; what needs to take place is a gradual casting-off of all that other people may want us to be in order to decide for ourselves who we are and what we stand for.

The truth is there's never been more pressure to present pieces of ourselves to different people in different contexts. Your work self is different from your home self. The person you are with your parents isn't the person your friends know you as. This disconnected way of being is too rooted in control. Our desire to control the way we show up in the world comes from a fear of being judged, and also the taboo around letting an expression of honest feeling anywhere near our professional selves. Despite vast improvements in equality for women in my lifetime, we are still encouraged to see our femaleness in opposition to maleness. This binary approach isn't just limiting, it undermines the potential for our female energy to have a depth and complexity that we need to explore. And given that we spend most of our waking lives at work, this is a lot of time to spend suppressing swathes of ourselves that we fear may not be office appropriate. Holding something of yourself back is a kind of defensiveness. And it's not healthy.

If you just exist from one scenario or drama to the next, you are a collection of experiences, and not a solid person. This is a recipe for insecurity, stress, anxiety and general dissatisfaction. It is the opposite of what it means to become a gentlewoman and show up consistently as your whole self in every aspect of your life.

I don't think it would be very gentlewomanly to claim to have mastered the art of being one. I have been broken, had to gather up pieces of myself and try to assemble them into a new form. I don't mean I was an emotional wreck – what I mean is more that my sense of my self was fractured. I was different things to different people and that made it easy not to be honest with them, and with myself. My life was compartmentalized and my emotions were too. I didn't like myself because I couldn't get a handle on myself as a whole. Lying in bed at night, in the darkness, I felt like I was floating, there was nothing to ground me. I was really scared that if I opened all the 'boxes' I had control of and let everything spill out together into the light – guilt, grief, anger, jealousy, sadness, anxiety – I would never be able to get myself back together. I was wrong. When my cousin Billie, who was more like an older sister to me, died aged just 31, I realized what a privilege and joy it is just to be alive. I owed it to her to give my life its best shot. So, I made a choice – I did not want the tragedies that befell my family, or my negative experience in a decade-long destructive relationship, to become my entire story.

I listened to the inner-person I'd aspired to be for so long and took back the narrative of my life. I began fitting all the fragments together into a whole picture rather than various incomplete ones. I started by being caring and patient with myself and others. I decided to project positivity into the world, and in response, good things started happening. My career took off, I broke free from that bad relationship, found real love, and one day I realized that this was what real happiness felt like for me. It became clear that

I had constructed a way of being that I was inhabiting rather than 'adopting' when, despite losing my dream job, and having just discovered my wife was pregnant, I was...fine. Nothing could shake the anchor I'd found inside myself. Challenges, tragedies, injustices are the stuff of life. I can't change that but the structure, balance, stability and positive mental attitude I've found by trying to be a gentlewoman will always help me handle it.

And now I want to share how possible it is to be a 'strong woman' through the use of our innate, soft power rather than by feeling the need to adopt a perceived 'tough' masculine performativity.

As you wake up each morning and check your phone, news from a turbulent world that appears to be hurtling towards destruction hits your homescreen and reminds you of that which you cannot control in life (unless you happen to be a global world leader reading this, in which case – carry on, and thank you). It's never been more important than it is now to know yourself and commit to being your own best friend and ally through life. Because our response to this world, and who we are in it, is the only thing we can truly have power over. If we are going to live longer than our mothers' generation, let's make the most of it. Let's live well and fully, be entirely present, and confident that by being a gentlewoman great happiness and success is ours for the taking.

Herein lies a 'gentle' antidote to the often brutal modern world.

CHAPTER 1

Being at home

The first thing I'm going to ask you to do as we fill the tank ready to go on this epic road trip together towards happiness, fulfilment and becoming a gentlewoman (don't worry, I've brought snacks), is to look around at where you live, or spend most of your time. When you put your key in the door do you feel happy to be back or a nagging dread?

'I don't want to own anything until I find a place where me and things go together,' says Holly Golightly in Truman Capote's *Breakfast at Tiffany's*.[1] But Holly is a lost soul, disconnected and endlessly performing a version of herself. She's so unsettled she can't even commit to naming her cat. She lacks stability and as a result she feels at home nowhere. It is so vital to have a strong sense of your roots, the things that attach you to your world and to your experience of life. Without these foundations you will be as insubstantial as Holly, forever a 'Miss Whoever-you-are'.

Have you ever walked into a building and felt instantly ill-at-ease? You can't quite put your finger on why but there's something that's just a bit off. The longer you spend in the space, the more your spirits drop. You know immediately, instinctively, if the house you're viewing is 'the one' or not. Get through the door and as the estate agent launches into a spiel about the fabulous ceiling height, you think, 'Nope. Next.' Hotel rooms are just as susceptible to the subtle vibration of negative energy as dentists' waiting rooms. Because this isn't about decor, it's about the deeper character of an environment and the intentions of the people who made it that way.

Our homes should be our sanctuary: somewhere that inspires us and makes us feel protected from the outside world. Whether it's a tiny rented flat above a kebab shop (been there, done that), or a suburban family house, you should never put up with a space that doesn't make you feel safe. It takes imagination, not money, to transform it. Your home truly is an outward reflection of your inner self, so identify what it is you are craving most – security, love, comfort or company, for example – and turn the place you live into somewhere that can give you all you need.

START BY MAKING YOUR BED EVERY DAY, NO MATTER HOW BUSY YOU ARE

If you are someone who thinks, 'What's the point if I'm out all day and will just get straight back into bed once I'm home', then I'd hazard a guess that this 'why bother' attitude has been born out of a sense that you don't deserve good things from yourself or others. But such a simple act of self-care sets you up not just for the next 24 hours, but for an entire approach to your life. This seemingly small act will help you to take more positive, self-orientated steps throughout the day – you have started as you mean to go on. Making your bed matters because *you* matter.

Gentle home hacks

OUT	IN
Wire coat hangers	Wooden hangers
Ugly chipped mugs	A matching set
Metal saucepans with burned bases	Ceramic pans
Dirty lace curtains	Shutters and blinds
Sagging mattress	Mattress topper
Bed pillows you've had for years	Goose down
Raggedy towels	Soft fluffy white towels
Dying spider plants	Fresh flowers
100-watt light bulbs	Smart light bulbs in softer, adjustable hues

You can fold your socks into perfect little Marie Kondo nuggets, curate your bathroom shelves so they are colour coordinated, and alphabetize your spice rack if you want, but these aren't really the things that you miss if you're away from home for a period of time, are they? What we long for is the mood or 'sense' of our space, the people we enjoy it with and the meaningful objects we fill it with. This is partly why Airbnb has become such a popular way to travel: we want to stay in spaces that are alive with the character and charm of the individual who created them.

Learn to appreciate the importance of putting the right kind of care into the place where you live. By that I mean flooding it with light as best you can (even if you live in a basement or have a wall in front of your window, there are always solutions). Also fill it with colour, things that make you smile, and areas where you can sit and think or entertain friends. Every gentlewoman's home has a place to eat that isn't the sofa and the table should fit as many people around it as possible. Because as Virginia Woolf wrote in *A Room of One's Own*: 'One cannot think well, love well, sleep well, if one has not dined well.'[2]

Would Virginia Woolf have ordered Deliveroo and eaten it in front of her favourite Netflix show (*RuPaul's Drag Race*?) from time to time, had such things existed in Bloomsbury London? Quite probably. Being a gentlewoman doesn't mean denying yourself occasional indulgences, but the benchmark for eating in, from which you allow yourself to deviate, should be enjoying a homemade meal, at the dining table, even if you are on your own. There is no better way to survey your queendom and enjoy actually living in your home rather than just existing in it in between leaving and getting back from work. We should aspire to create a nurturing environment where we can cast off the stresses of the day. Rather than crash out on the sofa, watching TV or staring at your phone when you get home, read a book in your favourite armchair, take a long bath, sit in the garden or have a glass of wine at the kitchen table. These are ways of taking good care of yourself by being truly present and engaged in your living space and giving yourself an opportunity to actually *be* at home.

When I feel the creeping sense that my days are not my own and people, work meetings, chores are all one big whirligig I'm losing my grip on, making a risotto in the kitchen makes me feel like I am back in the driving seat. As I splash a glug of white wine over the rice while it spits in butter and olive oil I regain that happy relationship with my home and with myself. Covering it in parmesan and adding another knob of butter, I close the lid of the pot and just plonk it on the dining table with a nice bottle of wine and a green salad, and everything seems right with the world again.

A gentlewoman's self-nourishing risotto recipe

Get a saucepan of vegetable stock simmering. Then in your best heavy-bottomed pan, melt a little butter and olive oil. Finely chop a large white onion, two cloves of garlic and a stick or two of celery and transfer to the pan. When soft add a mug of Arborio rice, stir it in the buttery oil for a hot minute or two then grab a half-drunk bottle of white wine and generously pour in. Wait until this has all been absorbed by the rice before gently ladling in the stock, stirring constantly until each spoonful of liquid has been absorbed. Put the radio on, fix yourself a drink – don't stop stirring! – and enjoy the process, it'll take about 30–40 minutes for the rice to be cooked, but use your judgement and add more stock if it's still too firm. Turn off the heat, grate a load of parmesan on top, cover. Serve with black pepper and extra cheese.

Cooking forces me to be in the moment. If I stop stirring the risotto it goes gloopy and is ruined. Handling ingredients, feeling the soft thud of a knife slicing an onion, the crack of garlic peeled from a clove, is the kind of physical experience I want after a day largely spent touching keyboards and screens. The 'internet of things' fills me with dread. I don't want a 'connected' home, I want to feel connected to my home, and having a fridge that tells me when I need milk is going to have the opposite effect. We now have apps to tell us when to breathe, when our period is going to start, when to leave the house to make an appointment on time, and yes – when we need to add things to a shopping list. These apps might make your life easier, but 'easy' isn't necessarily what a gentlewoman craves. Give her something real and meaningful instead. She would rather remain at one with her health, her body and the contents of her food cupboards than removed from them. Being domesticated doesn't sound very sexy but if it means owning my space and finding the most joy within my experience of it, then wrap me in an apron and call me Martha Stewart – I'm as domesticated as they come.

It's also so important to be in possession of the objects that will help facilitate your best home life, so vases, candles, good tablewear, napkins, wine glasses – all these things matter not as objects in themselves but as the experiences they represent. As the French existentialists decided over drinks in a Parisian café, 'You can talk about this apricot cocktail and make philosophy out of it!' For a gentlewoman, desiring to own or consume nice things is not about being materialistic, rather it is a kindness to yourself to enable the happy moments such objects signify.

Think of all the times you've had a great evening at someone else's house. You probably felt welcomed from the moment you stepped through the door; you were offered drinks, given somewhere comfortable to sit and left feeling jolly, a little flushed with wine but very well looked after. It is this kind of host that a gentlewoman should aspire to be. When my wife and I invite friends for dinner we put care and creativity into the experience. We plan the menu, cook, and make what I quite grandly call a tablescape but is in reality just a nicely laid table. If I have people in my home I take great pride in hosting them. There's nothing worse than feeling like you are encroaching on someone else's space. And there have been times when I've been invited into someone else's home only to understand that my presence there is a burden. Then the furniture, the pictures on the walls, the overhanging lights suddenly seem to loom over me whispering menacingly, 'You don't belong here.'

Things a gentlewoman has at home

- At least six wine glasses.
- Extra full set of bedding, spare toothbrush and towel.
- Yoga mat.
- First-class stamps.
- A ribbon and wrapping drawer.
- Teapot and cup set.
- Pack of cards.
- Bottle of whisky or other emergency stash.
- Full-length mirror by the door for yourself as much as guests.
- Fresh flowers or plants.
- A good bar of soap.
- A cushion that you love.

- Ambient lighting.
- A set of bowls.
- A spare gender-neutral dressing gown.
- Ice cubes in the freezer.

TO START LIVING AS A GENTLEWOMAN ENSURE YOU TRULY HAVE A ROOM OF YOUR OWN

This is non negotiable. Maybe you live alone, in which case revel in the opportunity not to have to accommodate someone else's collection of porcelain pigs. Most of us have to share our digs with friends, family or a partner, and in this case we must insist on a room, a corner, a coffee table or a shelf that is just ours, to represent our individual personality. No one else gets to put their things in, on or anywhere near this place because it is sacredly yours. When you look at it you are reminded of who you are and who you want to be. Think of it as a living Pinterest board you've entitled 'Me', complete with postcards, books, objects, letters, awards – anything that has a significant meaning for you, or inspires you in some way. What is the point of keeping all the mementoes of your life hidden away in boxes? Bring them out into the light for people to see, be proud of the stories they tell. These objects are the evidence of your reality so own them in every sense of the word.

Meet a gentlewoman

Brenna Hassett is an archaeologist who specializes in uncovering how people lived and died in the past.

What evidence is there that tribes of ancient people created 'sanctuaries' for themselves?

Our ancestors were highly mobile; it's only in the last 15,000 years or so (out of 300,000)[3] that humans have become 'sedentary'.[4] Once upon a time we may have been like mountain gorillas, building a new nest each night. What survives of these in the archaeological record are layers of ash from our fires; the pits and stone walls of our shelters; and even the microscopic traces of reed mats and the debris from everyday tasks like cooking and making stone tools.[5]

When did 'dwelling places' become more what we'd typically associate with a home?

Many of these shelters would have been temporary. However, people may have revisited certain locations over and over during their seasonal movements and some places might have been important touchstones (quite literally) in their lives. 'Home' for our species might have been found more in our social units, revisited and familiar landscapes, or even something more active, like taking part in a ritual. Many day-to-day tasks that we now think of as occurring at home (cooking, washing, making things) would possibly have been carried out in a public, common space, reflecting how societies may have shared resources in the past. The invention of more 'private space' may have gone along with changes in our society. Evidence from the archaeological site of Asikli Hoyuk in Turkey, for instance, shows that a bit more than 9,000 years ago, previously communal features like hearths moved inside to become parts of private 'households'.[6]

When and how did basic shelters turn into places with possessions and elements of decoration?
Personal decoration and possessions predate 'homes' by some margin...at least 40,000 years.[7, 8] It seems likely that we have always decorated our homes – there are traces of decorated plaster from many early villages across the ancient Near East going back at least 9,000 years.[9] And even before permanent houses, our shelter creations could be very artistic. Neanderthals are said to be responsible for some of the impressive mammoth-bone shelters found in Eastern Europe.[10]

As married or partnered lives merge, it's easy to lose track of what belongs to you and what is something you own together, and this I believe is a mistake. I'm not assuming you'll split up and abandon all your possessions, throwing just the bare essentials into a bin liner and leaving one night, never to return, as I did when I finally left my ex-partner. But I do think it's a mistake to entirely lose track of the things that belong just to you because once you do it's easier to lose track of yourself...and that is something a gentlewoman avoids like the 'Macarena' at a wedding reception.

The French philosopher Gaston Bachelard wrote in *The Poetics of Space*: 'The house shelters day-dreaming, the house protects the dreamer, the house allows one to dream in peace.'[11]

This is 'home' at its best, when your living space is a base from which you can fly. But when you lose confidence in yourself and are overwhelmed by the stresses of modern life, the first thing to slip through your fingers is normally the state of your home. Dishes pile in the sink, unopened letters stack up, nothing is put away and home becomes a place of conflict where you argue about chores with your partner, kids or flatmate. Because the kitchen isn't clean you don't like to cook in it, you order takeout and then stop even bothering with plates. If you think you don't deserve looking after, then why would you bother looking after your living space? The appearance of your home reflects your inner state of mind and self-worth. So when you start thinking things don't matter that's when they matter most. It goes back to the importance of making your bed every day: when you are at your worst, put your best freshly washed and ironed sheets on your bed. It's a small change but it can be the start of a new way of thinking and being kinder to yourself.

As more and more 'life' happens to me, I recognize the ability of the place where I live to anchor me to myself. My Aunt Vonnie died when I was 18. It was sudden and on the night of her brain haemorrhage, my mum drove to her house to pick up her daughter, my younger cousin Romy, who was just 11, and bring her back to ours. We lay a mattress on the floor of my bedroom for her that night and I found some of my old soft toys to tuck in with her, knowing in the morning she would find out that her mother was dead and her life would be changed for ever. In the weeks after it happened we were heavy with shock and just starting to feel the first pinpricks of grief. But I remember how my family home in those early days became a place of refuge – my mum bought big bunches of flowers and we had vases cascading with colour in every room. We opened all the windows so that fresh air and sunlight greeted every sad day and, when the night came, we lit candles so that there was always a sense that something magical might be happening. It is a gentlewoman's skill – maybe more a ritual or belief – to be able to keep a home full of light and life amid darkness.

Creating a good and happy home in this way can help us stay grounded and secure through the hardest times. It's so vital to be able to cultivate this 'belief' for yourself so that you are ready to find solace from your living space when you need it most and also enjoy welcoming others into the nurturing environment you have designed, to share in its warmth when they need it too. So much of being a gentlewoman is about getting yourself to a good place so you are best able to be a positive influence on others.

I find it disheartening, then, when people talk about going 'home' for the weekend, as if the life they are living in the city is just an extended holiday, an 'elsewhere' they inhabit between trips 'home'. The language of belonging changes by stealth, and there comes a time for most of us when we stop calling the place we are from 'home' without even realizing. It's not until this happens that we truly start becoming ourselves *for* ourselves. And while the memory of the place where you grew up remains stitched into the fabric of your life, you must let go of the emotional attachment to it in order to make space for a place of your own.

Your entire home should make you feel good when you're there alone and you should be proud to invite others over to share in the feeling with you, because it is people who really make a place seem alive with love and warmth and laughter and all that comes with it.

where you can totally belong in the world, and the cornerstone of life when everything else shifts and warps. At best it should provide gentle solace from the brutal realities of the world we live in.

Loss had been layered upon loss for me for such a long time – the death of my Aunt Vonnie and then a decade later the death of my beloved older cousin Billie, coupled with the shock of finding out, shortly before her death, that my dad was leaving my mum for another woman and my parents weren't the happy couple I'd thought they were, and then my own dysfunctional relationship. What had become of me? I wasn't sure. But it was time to find out. After finally breaking up with my ex, I moved into a tiny rented studio just off London's Portobello Road. This place was so small it just fitted a bed on a mezzanine, a microwave and a tiny well-designed shower room and toilet. I felt instantly at home and wasted no time in putting my stamp on it – covering the walls with postcards, photos and pages from magazines. This was the start of putting myself back together. Modern living isn't about creating a space that looks good on Instagram; it needs to feel good, no filter required.

When I woke up in my little flat every morning, I saw myself reflected back. It felt safe, vibrant and I had so much joy on my doorstep, living a stone's throw from a market, bars, restaurants and the bustle of real life. It was the happiest I'd been in years. As soon as I had this new base for myself, I reconnected with friends. I piled them in, and we ordered pizzas and turned the music up loud. We danced and drank wine and I felt free from all the rules that had previously stopped me from living life in Technicolor.

My new home was a turning point. It was also an example of how making one positive change can start the process of changing other things about yourself and your life. I realized how much contentment I could find in filling up my world with positive things.

The word 'space' can mean a gap, 'emptiness', or it can mean a place yet to be inhabited. We can choose to live in emotional deficit or we can add to and enrich our lives. I had agency for the first time in a long time and the choice I made then, to create a good, happy base for myself, was the groundwork I needed to do to start really engaging with the idea of the kind of woman I could become.

Things a gentlewoman can do herself at home

- Paint a room with minimal mess.
- Use a power drill.
- Erect flat-pack furniture with minimal stress.
- Put up shelves.
- Fix a dripping tap.

'Do It Yourself' is an ethos and way of thinking about your home and your life as much as it is a proficiency with a toolbox. Learn how to use a power drill, put up shelves, hang pictures, and move away from the person or thing dividing you from the life you want to live. Start building the home you deserve.

Gentle suggestions for how to be at home

- Make the bed every single day.
- Always have fresh flowers or plants in the house.
- Light candles in the evening but go easy with the scented ones to avoid the ambience feeling oppressively fragrant.
- Use napkins – if you have cloth napkins they should ideally be ironed (but who has the time!). Paper napkins are fine. Never kitchen roll, even if you're eating alone, and never EVER a bit of loo roll.
- Play music you love on a good speaker.
- Put art on the wall but only if it means something to you.
- Paint behind radiators.
- Never call a pro until you have watched at least one how-to YouTube video explaining how to fix it yourself.
- Don't put up too many photos of yourself, it gives the wrong impression.
- Sleep with the bedroom window open even in cold weather.
- Buy books, read them and keep them out to talk to other people about.
- Take your bathing ritual seriously, there's no point soaking for less than 20 minutes.

CHAPTER 2

Being a friend

Flakiness is the enemy of a gentlewoman:

Rain-checking;
Running really late (over half an hour);
Not responding to messages;
Cancelling at the last minute;
Never quite accepting invitations because you want to keep your options open;
...are ALL apparently acceptable behaviours today.

We have been trained to expect at least a third of our plans to veer off course, changing date, time and location and even cancelling them ourselves. In fact, there is a growing tendency to admit we love it when a friend cancels a plan, as if actually all we ever really want to do is sit alone with our phones, mindlessly double tapping their Instagram photos instead of bothering to spend time with them in real life. I'm here to tell you that this is *not OK*. Not even in the slightest. It is the antithesis of being a gentlewoman and symptomatic of the splintered, uncommunicative ennui of our hyper-connected world.

I agree, being reliable doesn't sound sexy, but for a gentlewoman it is one of the most important characteristics to cultivate. Making plans with friends and sticking to them unless there's a really good reason not to demonstrates kindness towards individuals you should care about and a profound respect for the relationships you have built with them. Also, let's not forget, spending time with someone who uplifts and inspires you, challenges you and makes you laugh, is one of life's great joys.

Capturing the difficulty of defining the love that exists in friendship, the poet Elizabeth Jennings writes:

Such love I cannot analyse;
It does not rest in lips or eyes,
Neither in kisses nor caress.
Partly, I know, it's gentleness[1]

If you truly dread following through with arrangements because you aren't looking forward to seeing the people you'd planned to see, then maybe it's time to think about why you are making arrangements with them in the first place. With real friends it's not enough to *say* you're friends, you have to *act* like it, and you can start by showing up, not flaking on them and your friendship.

In the digital age unreliability is at your fingertips, but perhaps if you had to pick up the phone to explain why you suddenly couldn't make a date that had been in the diary for months, you might think twice about it. Instead, you can hide behind a WhatsApp message, replacing remorse with a sad-face emoji. Technology allows us to avoid the reality of human emotion, but unless we really hear the disappointment in someone's voice or see the flicker of irritation in their eyes we don't ever really feel the consequences of our cancelling.

I have the kind of friends who like to make plans and stick to them, and it's rewarding to feel as though I'm surrounded by people who put as much effort as I do into maintaining and growing our friendships. If you are a gentlewoman, or on your way to becoming one, you should be eager to look after the relationships that matter most by staying in regular touch and thinking of imaginative things to enjoy together. It can be simple acts of kindness to yourself first, that help create the base from which you are best placed to care for others.

This might sound a bit 'Minecraft', but design a world around you that you *want* to inhabit. Just make sure those walls aren't so high that friends can't reach you when you need their support. Remember, a good life is not a single-player game.

WHAT KIND OF FRIEND ARE YOU?

Giver

You might wonder, if you stopped texting and calling friends, if you didn't invite anyone over, or out, how long it would be before your friends planned anything for you. But forget it, it doesn't matter. You should like your friends enough to trust that they aren't taking advantage of you. Think the best of people and adjust your expectations. Instead of wishing others were more like you, own and enjoy being a giver. If you are the person in a friendship group considered Organizer in Chief then as long as you are getting something back in return, my advice is not to fight it.

Receiver

If, on the other hand, you are someone who finds they are always just invited to stuff and never need arrange anything themselves, lucky you. And to you I say: be more gentlewoman. Reach out to others as much as they lean in to you (LA speak for 'make contact and make a plan') and see if you enjoy feeling like a more accomplished and caring human being for it.

Avoider

You more often than not find it hard committing to everything your friends suggest. You'll be running out of excuses soon for why you can't make it this time, so best to initiate a break-up and figure out how and where to find 'your people'.

One of the most over-used excuses for not putting as much time and effort into friendships as you should is being 'too busy'. If you're a surgeon working a 15-hour shift, who also happens to be a single mum with four kids, two dogs, an elderly mother in a care home, a role on the board of a charity and a triathlon to train for, then yes, you *are* busy, but most of us over-dramatize what I would just call 'life' so that we are apparently drowning under our to-do lists. Be inspired by women such as Jacinda Ardern, the Prime Minister of New Zealand. Now, *she's* busy, running a country, looking after a new baby, generally being a good egg, etc., but she and countless other high-achieving women like her still manage to find time for themselves and their loved ones without, at least from this distance, looking like they are falling apart. If they can manage, us Muggles must be able to.

Meet a gentlewoman

Silvia Bellezza is a professor at Columbia Business School who has conducted research into the modern concept of busyness. She talked to me about her findings.

'A busy and overworked lifestyle, rather than a leisurely lifestyle, has become an aspirational status symbol. A series of studies shows that the positive inferences of status in response to busyness and lack of leisure are driven by the perceptions that a busy person possesses desired human capital characteristics (competence, ambition) and is scarce and in demand on the job market.

Brands appealing to people's lack of time could be a form of flattery, making them feel their time is very valuable. Feeling busy and overworked may make us feel more valuable and important. Targeting busy and pressed-for-time consumers has also proven to be a rewarding strategy for sellers of products originally conceived for other markets and sold for other benefits. For instance, coders, engineers and venture capitalists are increasingly turning to liquid meals and powdered drinks so they can more quickly get back to their computer work. The demand in Silicon Valley for these products, originally catering to athletes and dieters, is so high that some report being put on monthly waiting lists to receive their first orders. Another example is the print ad by Rolex that asks: 'Checking his watch costs Bill Gates $300 a second, what is your time worth?' Rather than flattering consumers' purchase ability and financial wealth, brands can flatter their busyness and lack of valuable time to waste'.

'How are you?'

'So busy!!!'

…has become a standard question/answer; as if having too much on is a kind of status symbol. Like Bill Gates's Rolex, it is a perceived emblem of power we think we hold over others. I believe it is quite the opposite. If what you feel more than anything else – more than 'happy' or 'inspired' or 'content' – is 'busy', then stop, take a breath and reassess how you manage your life. We need to reframe how we perceive busyness so it's not a frantic and out-of-control source of value.

For a start, if you were to take a closer look at what takes up your most valuable currency – time – then I bet there are quite a few things that you're doing for the wrong reasons and can redistribute. I could encourage you to get comfortable with the letters 'n' and 'o', as a way to minimize the plethora of tasks that can come to define our 'busy' lives if we are not careful. There are whole books and inspirational talks about why it is important for women to feel confident in saying 'no' more often. And I get it, there is a tendency for us to be natural people-pleasers and overly conscientious, especially in jobs in which we are so keen to *prove* our worth. Flexing our 'no' muscle is one response to millennia of being taken advantage of and having to constantly strive for opportunities in our personal and professional lives. But there is another, softer way. Because a 'hard no' – unless it's being shouted at a child about to crawl into a fire, or at a grown-up with wandering hands – is too blunt a rebuttal to satisfy a gentlewoman's need for positive, affirmative action rather than negative inaction. There are times when we use 'no' as a defence mechanism to protect ourselves from unpredictability or situations we don't have complete control over. We turn down work, social engagements, chances to travel, or even ordering pudding. But when you are next tempted to quickly dismiss something, challenge yourself – is it an opportunity to grow, to indulge yourself or simply have some fun? As Anaïs Nin wrote: 'Life shrinks or expands in proportion to one's courage.[2]

Instead of ruling something out entirely, a gentlewoman makes the effort to reframe the offer. Rather than resorting to 'no', try reframing it into a 'yes, but'.

SO, YES, BUT...

I'll need a longer deadline.

Not this weekend.

Can we meet earlier?

Can I have help?

It's easier if we do it earlier or closer to home.

I'm not coming in fancy dress.

You can pay me back in instalments.

Please don't @ me.

Just saying 'no' to opportunities and experiences can seem like the easy option as it means you don't have to negotiate anything potentially complicated or be honest about how you feel and why your instinct is to deny the request or opportunity. Instead, think about what you'd need to do in order to make the ask work for you, and if it definitely isn't going to *ever* work for you then, of course, a polite but firm 'no thank you' does remain an option.

Be the high-powered CEO of your own social life; introduce new ways of working, objectives and values, but be your best kind of boss. Start by buying a proper full-week-view diary and take it everywhere with you. Calendars on your phone are useful, but it's easy to feel less connected to your week ahead if it's all behind a screen. And with alerts beeping throughout the day, it can seem as if your iCal is in charge of you, not vice versa.

Take back control of your time and review your diarized plans often, looking closely for anything that you have coming up that you are completely dreading. Don't put off thinking about it until the day before, because that is when bad habits kick in and you send a panicky text cancelling because you just can't face it, citing 'work emergency', 'family/flatmate issue' or 'pet crisis'. Something about the act of writing an appointment in your diary makes you more responsible for it and having to cross or rub things out when plans change is a reminder of the impact this has on others more than just swiping 'delete' and being absolved.

Extricate yourself from the arrangement with ample time, and face up to the reason why you don't want to do it. Be honest about your commitment struggle and examine what it is that is preventing you from wanting to see that person or be sociable at all. Women are twice as likely as men to suffer from anxiety and this should make it easier to be truthful; if you are suffering from a psychological issue or nervousness after a challenging period of your life, explain to people why you need to pull out of something. 'I have anxiety and today has been a hard day, I'm just not feeling up to it' is far easier for whomever you are 'letting down' to understand than a shoddy made-up excuse. Choose honesty and straightforwardness in every interaction and you will feel an emotional burden lifted from your shoulders.

I have a colour code in my diary for the different demands on my time, and there's a hierarchy of importance. Family comes first, then self-care, then work, then friends. This order has shifted at different times over the years; it has even shifted week to week, depending on what's going on at that time.

Quickly sketch a circle and divide it into segments plotting how much of your time is taken up with:

Family;

Work;

Friends;

Time for yourself.

Naturally all our charts will differ and shift over time too but it is those of you for whom work takes up the biggest slice of your life that I'm most concerned for. There are times when we're working on something we feel so proud and passionate about that we positively choose it to be the most important thing in our diary that week. But looking after yourself should be more of a priority. Personally, I'm better at everything else when I've given myself some time. It could be as no-frills as scheduling in a walk to work, or getting to the gym. I am a more successful friend when I take this time for myself and work it into my life in a functional way. What I strive for in a week is a good balance of all the different colours in my diary and if it's looking too weighted in one direction or another I'll make some phone calls and rejig accordingly.

Gentlewomen filter their friendships, so they waste no effort maintaining one-sided relationships. Take a look at the people who you surround yourself with and if any so-called friends bring you down or fill your time with histrionics and neediness, you may want to consider kindly but firmly letting them go. A gentlewoman devotes a lot of herself, her efforts and her energy to the people closest to her and it's so important that these dynamics work both ways, if they don't the effect is depleting. You have limited resources and you must learn where and how best to deploy them.

If time is your most valuable asset, then a big drain on this can be someone who has held on to the space they take up in your life because you've known each other a long time but have very little that actually connects the two of you any more. Taking action can feel like having to dump a lover, but it doesn't need to be as heart wrenching. My advice would be to exercise caution when acquiring new friendships in the first place as these can often be the ones you regret taking from the friendly acquaintance zone – which, might I add, is a perfectly acceptable place to keep people such as neighbours or that nice woman at yoga – into something more committed. Do not say 'we must go for coffee' to someone out of politeness unless you would genuinely get some pleasure from the experience and intend to follow through.

A friend evaluation sounds a little *Hunger Games* but it is a way of remaining conscious and engaged with the networks you have formed. As you grow they shift, people change, worlds don't align any more and your reliance on each other may just naturally lessen over time. Taking gentle care of yourself in the context of your social life means being aware of when to salvage a friendship and when to let it go.

So, how best to part ways with someone who may have once been a friend but no longer behaves like one and drags you down or takes advantage of you? Well, unfortunately there's no one right answer and a gentlewoman should put the requisite amount of thought into what the kindest approach, and the one least likely to cause conflict, would be. Perhaps if you've been friends since school, you owe it to the longevity of your relationship to meet in person and discuss the fact that your lives have gone in different directions or maybe the issue is that you need time off from your connection as you are finding it has a negative impact on your life.

Alternatively, leave the WhatsApp group (more on how to do this like a gentlewoman in Chapter 9), unfollow them on social media, and assume they'll get the hint, if that will save their pride in the long run.

I trust that you know who is worth persevering with and who isn't. We all go through difficult times that make us less good friends, so it's important not to cut someone out of your life unless you really feel it is for the best. As a gentlewoman you are empathetic and emotionally intelligent enough to know when someone needs you and equally when you need to move on.

Meet a gentlewoman

Heather Havrilesky is *New York Magazine*'s legendary agony aunt 'Ask Polly'.

What are the biggest issues facing friendship today?
I think most people struggle to ask their friends for exactly what they need – our culture also perpetuates the myth that the ideal is not to rely on or lean on other people in any kind of way that might inconvenience them. If you are doing that, you are a little bit pathetic and are failing in some way. We don't treat each other as inter-dependent, connected parts of the community that much any more: we act like if you need help somehow that is a moral failing on your part.

What do you think is the kindest way to break up with a friend?
Oh God. It's tough, because our culture would say you ghost them – you just drop out of their lives and don't say anything. With new

friendships, it's a little bit odd to say, 'Well, I know we have just become friends, but I don't want you in my life, I've just decided.' I feel like the most humane thing is just to tell someone directly that the friendship isn't working, but without stigmatizing them or making it somehow about their flaws.

What do you think are some of the warning signs that a friendship isn't working for you any more?

For me it is examining the level of contempt you have after seeing someone. Do you feel satisfied? Do you laugh together? Are you honest with each other? I think that you can kind of see walls coming up sometimes and feel that the honesty is gone and there is not enough joy – leading to a question of: 'Why are we continuing this?' There is a feeling you can have when you are driving away from seeing someone when you think, 'What did I just do?' I do think that sometimes the issue is that you feel like you have not really been there or have been serving this person without really getting what you need – and vice versa.

WHO ARE WE RESPONSIBLE FOR?

Air travel affords us with some good life lessons: a gin and tonic can help when things get turbulent, watching *Bad Moms* is always a good idea, and most importantly put your own oxygen mask on before helping others with theirs. There's a lot of truth in this ubiquitous safety message; I take it to mean, once you've got yourself sorted, you are better able to think of others. Are they really OK? Social media can make us feel connected to friends – we know what holidays they've been on, see pictures of their home life and work –

but do we really know what's going on? Pick up the phone and call one of your friends, someone you've not spoken to or seen for a while even if you message most days. Do it now: call them. It's so important to check in with each other's mental health, ask questions and not just assume because they posted a highly liked flat lay of their breakfast this morning it means they are happy (more often than not, if they are posting incessantly, they are seeking validation because they are unhappy).

In a letter to his girlfriend, the poet Philip Larkin, who has never really struck me as Mr Popular, wrote: 'I sometimes wonder if anyone can do anything for anyone'[3]

I think he's wrong. We must look out for each other, we have a responsibility to our friends and we should not underestimate our power to change their lives for the better.

We all make judgements too quickly on people; a two-second look and then a left or right swipe is what we afford other humans nowadays, so it's no wonder we are in this 'judge or be judged' era. I confess that this has affected me, too: I am bored easily by anyone who tells rambling anecdotes with no punchline, or doesn't ask any questions or offer interesting opinions, or who seems negative and low energy. I like to be amused and swept off my feet by someone's charm within minutes of meeting them or I can quite quickly decide, 'I have enough friends, thanks.' But in an effort to become more of a gentlewoman I have tried to be what I have termed 'mindfully judgey'.

We should be open-minded and actively seek to diversify our friendship groups by engaging with people outside our usual cliques and covens. But equally it's OK to be confident in knowing what you want and need from a BFF, an FF or indeed just an F, and not waste time on those you don't vibe with. I want to surround myself with people who make me feel good. They mustn't be dull, instead make plans, be inquisitive, offer advice, listen but also talk openly about themselves. I need friends I can be silly with and friends I can be serious with, and I believe the best kind of friends can do both.

Gossip, according to a dictionary definition, is 'the unsanctioned evaluative talk about people who aren't present' – but it can be such fun! The challenge for a gentlewoman is not to allow the fact that you are naturally inquisitive and love telling a good story to spill into spending the social currency of other people's secrets, because although it might afford you some short-term kudos, it'll leave you morally bankrupt. I believe we should also try not to talk about someone we don't wish well, or revel in *schadenfreude*. Meanness about others is something a gentlewoman prefers to avoid. It's dangerous to only get a sense of your own worth and power from denigrating someone else. This doesn't make you a Dorothy Parker of a wit, but a bully. If a group of friends are having a kiki that turns into a bitching session, don't engage. You don't need to kill the party or be sanctimonious but you also don't need to get drawn in and brought down. Walk away from these kinds of conversation with your head held high and be mindful of when camp, sass or comedic sending-up veers into cruelty.

There are definite rights and wrongs in romantic partnerships:
- Don't have it off with other people (unless previously agreed);
- Stay in regular contact with each other (the sending of cat gifs is optional but encouraged);
- Share future plans and social lives;
- Perform thoughtful gestures;

- Celebrate anniversaries;
- Surprise each other with presents;
- Speak on the phone.

Friendships, however, come with no such rulebook. But does the lack of a predefined structure for platonic relationships mean there is no such thing as being a good or a bad friend, seeing as how we're all just messing around in the sandpit of life, hoping someone will share their bucket with us? No. There may not be a contract in the same way there is for a marriage, but friendships still come with their own boundaries and expectations, we're just creating them for ourselves and constantly renegotiating the terms according to circumstance and instinct. And this is what makes having friends so precious and the ways we tend to these friendships of such importance.

A gentlewoman should try to mix friendship groups without worrying about people 'not getting on'. As you become more confident in yourself and the person you want to be, you'll surround yourself with friends who embody the same kind of values and characteristics as you. And you'll have learned by now when it's worth persevering and when to let go of the people who aren't good for you, so there will be something beyond superficial interests or professions that they'll all have in common.

Introduce your family to your friends – invite friends to family events and invite family to appropriate occasions with your friends. I believe gathering people together and exploring each other's connections is a way of not segregating yourself into 'work-self', 'home-self', 'childhood-self', 'school-self' and 'relationship-self', which is ultimately limiting and unfulfilling. Throwing these parts of your 'self' together, along with the people who know you within each segment, allows you to live a more rounded and whole existence, rather than a compartmentalized one. This community of friends from disparate pockets of your life is your adult existence. Connect your dots and a clearer illustration of yourself will emerge.

Elizabeth Jennings again:

Two people, yes, two lasting friends.
The giving comes, the taking ends.
There is no measure for such things.
For this all Nature slows and sings.

My ex-partner made it clear she didn't like my friends. It was often easier to turn down an invite to a party than discuss going. If I stayed home I'd hate myself, but if I went I'd spend the whole time worrying about how she was feeling. I think more of us than we'd like to admit will have at times sacrificed our friends for our lover. But this is never right. No one should choose between a closeness to them or a closeness to your friends. The best partners want to get to know your friends because your friends are a part of you.

In the weeks after leaving my ex-girlfriend, I felt euphoric. I would stay out as late as I wanted with friends, I would go away for the weekend at the drop of a hat with them, I would sleep over at their houses – I was free to engage with how important this group of people were to me.

I realized my life had been an archipelago; now all these separate islands were becoming, to quote John Donne, 'a piece of the continent, a part of the main'.[4]

A gentlewoman chooses to put time and effort into maintaining friendships because if what Aristotle said was true (and let's face it, it often was) that: 'A friend is a second self…consciousness of a friend's existence makes us more fully conscious of our own'[5], then building solid, meaningful friendships is at the root of being your best self. In order to do this, take your friendship offline and into the real world. You may meet online – and how wonderful that Instagram and other social media platforms can introduce us to like-minded people – but arrange a get-together IRL before it gets too weird to bother. A gentlewoman does not count her Twitterati or most ardent Insta commenters as friends unless she has their phone number, knows their star sign and has met for at least three actual dates. This does not mean that sliding into each other's DMs isn't a kind of relationship, it is, it's just not a real friendship and as such should be afforded less of your energy. If you like this person's online persona enough then invest in making it real.

According to much quoted research by Robin Dunbar, the director of the Institute of Cognitive and Evolutionary Anthropology at Oxford University, human beings have a finite capacity to maintain meaningful relationships with 150 people. This is now known as Dunbar's number.[6] His findings also suggest humans have on average:

5 intimate friends;

15 best friends;

50 good friends;

150 friends;

500 acquaintances and…

1,500 people we recognize on sight.

He says: 'The 150 layer is the important one: this defines the people you have real reciprocated relationships with, those where you feel obligations and would willingly do favours.'

A gentlewoman, however, is more interested in those five intimate and 15 best friends and putting her social efforts into these people. Devote half an hour every Sunday evening to making plans to see them. Think of experiences you can have together that suit the nature of your friendship or that person's particular interests. Think of these as 'dates' and put in as much creativity as you would if you were trying to impress a new lover. How about a walk somewhere neither of you has been before and a pub lunch? Or going to a museum, an antiques market, seeing if there's a free talk on somewhere that looks interesting? If it's your turn to organize then do a good solid job, look up places online in advance to make sure they're deserving of your patronage, check that it's on or open and buy tickets in advance. All these things might sound a bit dull, but they make for more seamless fun times, meaning you can concentrate on being together, rather than trying to find somewhere to get a sandwich.

For many women today, our friends are the most important and long-standing relationships in our lives. And yet we rarely put as much thoughtfulness, care and consideration into these partnerships as we do our romantic flings. I want to encourage you to think differently and demonstrate how much friends mean to you more often.

Write a list of your 15 favourite people, to borrow from Dunbar. Get out your diary – the paper one you now carry with you no matter how heavy it makes your handbag – and schedule something with each of them over the next three months. When we're all so 'BUSY!!!' it's the only way to stay really connected. I am also an advocate for treating your friends to tokens of your affection. Send flowers out of the blue, write letters, find out what restaurant they are celebrating their wedding anniversary in, phone up and arrange for two glasses of fizz to be sent to their table.

Are you someone who thinks you don't get on with other women, proudly proclaiming that you much prefer the company of men? If so, alarm bells should be ringing. Ask yourself honestly what it is about female energy that repels you, because it suggests that maybe there's something about your own femininity that you aren't comfortable with, and you will never be a gentlewoman if this is the case. Certainly when I felt that I didn't connect with women, it was in part because as a queer person I was still figuring out how to reconcile my desire for women with my presentation of myself as a woman. But gentlewomen today don't need to conform to any preconceived notions of womanhood. Your gender and sexuality are yours for the taking; define them, or don't define them, as you wish. There is strength in what makes you 'not a man', and that is to be used by you, on your own terms.

We live in a patriarchy where, traditionally, let's call them 'yin' characteristics, are sidelined by the more pushy 'yang' in our endless quest to be happy and successful. It is through embracing gentleness, and softening those hard yangy edges, nuzzling into the bosom of our friendships rather than appropriating a way of being that celebrates a 'hell is other people' masculine individualism, that allows us to reap the emotional benefits of really meaningful relationships.

I've been both an A+ and a Must Try Harder friend, with different people and at different times with the same person. And I'm so grateful that my very best friends didn't dump me when I neglected them for years as I was so deeply tangled up with grief and limited in every way by a no-good relationship. Those feelings consumed me then and left little space for me to think of anyone else.

I realize now that a happy life is a joined-up life, where all those bits of ourselves we feel the need to keep packaged up separately – because of insecurity, defensiveness or, in some cases, survival – are tipped out together into one big fabulous sprawling mess. Try undoing all the unnecessarily complicated knots which you feel are keeping the different parts of your life in place. Do this by opening yourself up in every way, letting everyone in, and not worrying about the consequences…because it takes things falling apart for things to fall into place.

Gentle suggestions for being a friend

- Reply to an invitation within 24 hours.
- Plan ahead. Think of something a particular friend will love and arrange to do it a month from now.
- Say yes more than no.
- Send thank-you cards. A text in an UBER home won't suffice.
- Arrive five minutes early if you arrange to meet someone out.
- Arrive 11 minutes late if you are going to their house.
- Don't bring elderflower cordial to a friend's house because you personally aren't drinking. Your host might still appreciate some wine.
- Never stay any later than 5.30pm if you are invited to a friend's house for lunch.
- Make time to talk to and connect with your friends' children. Ask them questions or engage with them on their level.
- Mix friendship groups – true contentment comes from having a joined-up life, not keeping people in separate boxes.
- Speak on the phone but don't leave voicemails.
- Be conscious of your friends' financial health and only make plans everyone can afford.
- Tell your best friends you love them.

CHAPTER 3

Being alone

What's the worst thing that can happen if you're eating in a restaurant on your own?

The maître d' suggests you wait till your 'friend' arrives?

People think you have no friends or have been stood up?

You're ignored by the waiter?

You get bored?

How about you spectacularly set fire to the menu?

...because this *actually* happened to me. It was one of those pompously oversized menu cards and as I scanned it for something treat-worthy (whenever I dine out alone I compensate for the lack of company with indulgent food choices) I smelled burning. Having no one sitting opposite me to intervene, and being in the kind of happy, introspective trance I fall into when I'm alone, I didn't notice that the table candle had licked the edge of the entrées and that while I was deciding if I'd have frites on the side, the whole thing was ablaze. A quick-thinking sommelier doused it in a bottle of San Pellegrino and disaster was averted, but not before I had the attention of everyone in the restaurant.

I find it best to 'own' embarrassing situations, to say 'yep, that was me, that happened', and defuse the moment with humour. On the whole we humans are rooting for each other and while *schadenfreude* does exist, it's rare that we really relish seeing a complete stranger fail (or set fire to the restaurant you are in).

The worst thing I could have done in that moment was avoid eye contact, shrink into my seat and order the bill, vowing never to eat in a fancy restaurant on my own again – look what happens! Instead, I smiled at the staring faces. 'Show's over, I'm afraid,' I said with a laugh as I moved to a clean table, ordering three courses and an extra-large glass of wine before returning to my book. I made the situation OK for my fellow diners. I showed them that I was someone who could handle the embarrassment with a wry laugh and was so comfortable in my skin, I wouldn't bow to public humiliation.

If something like this occurs when you're on your own it can feel infinitely worse than if you have someone by your side to share in the awkwardness or to tell you it wasn't that bad…honest. Plus, it's always easier to perform your most cool and confident, 'totally not bothered' self when you have a co-star to bounce off. But try being this version of you without a foil. Life gets so much easier when you are as confident alone as you are with others. There are no limits to what experiences can be enjoyed minus a plus one.

When people tell me they don't like being on their own, I can't help thinking they're doing it wrong. I've interviewed many celebrities in my job as a magazine journalist who tell me they can't cope with being alone. What does that say about them? Well, I think it means they don't have a solid sense of self and rely too much on their personality being constructed and reflected back at them by their 'friends' – the teams of managers, publicists and general life fluffers who are constantly in their orbit. Some of the really famous people I've spent time with for work have a hall of mirrors in their legions of fans, whose distorted idea of the celebrity can often be inseparable from the celebrity's idea of themselves and that's a dangerous place to be. Now social media makes us all celebrities of a sort and anyone with Instagram is at risk of developing the same kind of insubstantial personality constantly seeking validation, attention and likes.

Ask yourself a simple question: *Who am I in the dark, when no one's looking?* Learn to be proud of this person, to like them and trust them. You are your constant companion so be loyal to yourself. This will then underpin and secure everything else you do to create your image in the light of day – from the clothes you wear to the pictures you post. These things will enrich rather than define you.

Novelist and consummate gentlewoman Olivia Laing wrote:

> *I don't believe the cure for loneliness is meeting someone, not necessarily. I think it's about two things: learning how to befriend yourself and understanding that many of the things that seem to afflict us as individuals are in fact a result of larger forces of stigma and exclusion, which can and should be resisted.*[1]

Assuming that having a partner means you automatically get a sense of belonging is a big mistake. A relationship that doesn't allow you to flourish or be truly 'seen' by the other person is, in fact, much worse than being single, when at least you don't have to constantly second guess yourself or measure your actions and responses all the time. Likewise, being around lots of people when you don't feel part of the crowd can be truly alienating if you can't naturally find a way to occupy your own space in it. Equally, some people are in such emotionally dependent relationships, all they do is talk to each other about what they are thinking and feeling until they merge into one amorphous 'bae'*. We all know couples who believe they are greater than the sum of their parts and they seem to forget who they are separately.

A gentlewoman should think of herself as an individual inside and outside of a relationship. Never – not even after a rom-com binge or the best sex of your life – say to a lover, 'You complete me.' *Complete yourself!*

Invest time in learning to answer your basest emotional needs. Not only will this make you stronger in a relationship but it will mean if you separate you are not entirely destroyed by heartbreak. The period after a break-up can be the loneliest many of us experience, but if you have 'befriended' yourself it will make it easier to move on as you still have yourself by your side.

Enabling change in your life takes work. And that's not work you can do alone. You need to ask for help. It's through dialogue that your outlook on life will slowly, subtly shift.

Being in control of your own narrative, through the act of talking about it to friends or a therapist, allows you to free yourself from constraints you have built around your life. I found the courage to leave my ex by thinking about how I'd explain my decision to my therapist. Having someone 'witness' my life choices in this way broke the fourth wall of the unhappy microcosm my ex and I inhabited, and it helped set me free.

* bae = 'before anyone else'.

After a decade-long unhappy relationship, I vowed never to allow myself to feel so diminished by a relationship again. In talking to someone I didn't know (the joy of paying for therapy is you never need ask them anything about themselves) I remembered how good it felt to talk to people I did have a more emotionally reciprocal relationship with. So, I started to rebuild relationships with the friends and family I'd withdrawn from, by scrolling through my phone book and pressing 'call'. Not many answered (because everyone hates the intimate distance of phone calls these days, preferring the distant intimacy of messaging), but actually there was something crucial I had to do first.

It was time to learn to like myself.

I started by going to bars on my own, just to sit and read or watch the world go by. It's a habit I try to maintain as much as I can to this day. Hotel bars are great spots to go to alone as they aren't packed full of groups of mates out on a bender. Good ones are the right level of buzzy and there's a liminal sense of travellers just passing through that brings a liberating anonymity to the vibe. I decided that an 'Old Pal' would be my signature drink, because it often isn't on menus and I enjoy the nod a good mixologist gives me when I order it. Plus, it's a sipper, which is what you want when you're drinking alone, or before you know it you're slumped over a fourth Aperol Spritz having downed them like soda. There's nothing self-empowering about falling off a bar stool. Trust me.

Recipe for an Old Pal

Ingredients: Equal parts Cocchi Americano Bianco, rye whiskey, Campari.

Preparation: Stir together in a glass with one large rock of ice or several standard-sized ice cubes.

Served: Stirred.

Standard garnish: Lemon twist.

Drinkware: Lowball tumbler.

Choose a seat up at the bar if there is one, for optimum people-watching and some light conversation with the staff. It means you can be happily solo but also in the thick of it, which is preferable to staring at an empty chair opposite you. I'd also suggest taking a stack of papers and magazines or a book to read but make it something you'll enjoy, not something you think you'll look good reading as then the whole experience becomes awkward and contrived. And try really hard not to check your phone the entire time. This is 'you' time to be present with yourself not to focus on the lives of others. Use it as an opportunity to explore your autonomy, independence, apartness from people while also being part of the flow of life. Allow yourself the privilege of focusing on your day, your desires, your future plans. Such moments are an opportunity to contemplate without distraction the life that we have lived and construct a sense of the life we *want* to live. It allows us the time to move on while also accepting where we have started out from and what we have dealt with along the way. It is the best Tinder date you've never had.

Soon enough, I discovered that me, myself and I got on rather well because I had chosen to spend good, productive time on my own as well as open myself up completely to my friends and family with whom I had lots of fun and thought-provoking conversations. I had started to engage meaningfully with my own life too. I had finally become the protagonist of my story. Being happy alone has helped me get closer to becoming the kind of gentlewoman I have long aspired to be.

Dating, divorced, still not met anyone who deserves you? See this as an opportunity to enjoy your own company while filling your life with friends and happy family occasions. Don't agree to work late or at weekends because your colleagues have children and you don't; your time is equally valuable. Get that diary out again and hold back at least two nights a week for yourself.

A gentlewoman's warning

I am not exalting the 21st-century cult of 'just do you' (at the expense of anyone else) that encourages solipsism and selfishness. Yes, we are better, more thoughtful and productive people when we take time out for ourselves, but it should never be instead of our duty to those close to us. Understand this and reconcile what you must do for others with what you must do for yourself. It can take wiliness and imagination to make this balance of self and other work in every complicated life situation, and it's when you'll most need to know when to say either a 'yes but' or a mindful 'no' even to ostensibly inconsequential things.

We are bombarded with things we could or should do, things we must buy, places we need to go, podcasts to listen to, unseen TV, unheard new music, distant friends to message, family to FaceTime, an ever-growing number of unread emails and unretrieved voicemails…The world feels as though it is constantly playing that Hot Chip song 'do it do it do it do it do it do it do it now'[2] on repeat.

Having spare time is a luxury not to be wasted. I suggest really interrogating what experience you would get most out of and then committing to being fully present while enjoying that one activity rather than multitasking and frittering different pieces of yourself away doing various disparate things at the same time.

We should master the art of focus, or else it's so easy to become a total scatterbrain. I know when I'm feeling stressed or anxious because I begin to misplace my possessions. Some I can re-find, others I write off as just another unexplained disappearance brought on by trying to do too much with too little time.

In *The Psychopathology of Everyday Life*, Sigmund Freud wrote: 'We never lose what we really want.'[3] (But I bet Freud never left his Saint Laurent clutch bag in an airport lounge.)

When faced with a choice about how to spend your time, ask yourself: would being around friends lift your spirits, would a bit of online shopping do the job, or could helping your mum clear out her loft be a bit of a bore but make a big difference to her…or is this simply an opportunity to have a productive moment alone, away from people and your devices? Rather than answering emails while watching a TV show or taking a call during dinner or doing your online grocery shopping in a work meeting, try more often to employ unadulterated focus. Being entirely in the moment with something, whether you're alone or have company, is good for your soul.

Something I did discover during that prolonged period of me time was that I actually enjoy exercising, and if I do it alone I can find that steely focus I'm talking about. Running, for me, is a time to meditate, not breathlessly try to gossip with a mate while maintaining a steady 12-minute mile. And I don't need a personal trainer to waste half my session talking about the club night he's DJing at; in fact, I don't want to talk to anyone at all. I want to completely switch off and be so in it that I don't think about anything. I am all body, all sweat, all blood pumping, heart beating, and it's in this state that I feel like I'm really getting to know my true self and what I'm capable of. Even in a group class you survive by looking deep within yourself for every last resource of strength, and over time these profoundly personal physical experiences build up into a good strong core (and I don't just mean your abs).

'Conscious movement' was defined in an article by Stephanie Marsh in the *Guardian* as:

> *The idea that, if you're 'conscious', you're doing whatever it is that you're doing to your body with precision and a full awareness of the physical mechanisms at work – yin yoga is conscious, rugby is not.*
>
> *More importantly, it's also about being self-aware enough to see the big picture, diagnosing your physical, spiritual and emotional needs.*[4]

Placing responsibility for your sense of well-being on anything outside yourself – be that the number of Instagram followers you have, that work project that needs to be perfect or, yes, the calories you burned at a spin class – is a warning sign that you are trying to fill a nagging sense that something is missing from your life with the wrong thing. What a gentlewoman takes from this is that maybe doing Barry's Bootcamp every other evening isn't what she needs to be gentle to herself. I realized that doing too many HIIT classes and too much cardio was making me even more stressed. I was tired because I was waking up so early to train, my skin was dull, my under-eye circles almost ghoulish and my muscles ached because I didn't give them enough of a break. But I was my desired weight! And I enjoyed the smug feeling of accomplishment I got as I hoovered up a Skinny B*tch Smoothie after class. Does this sound familiar to you? If so, be kinder to yourself and swap your more intense training regimes for something gentler. Yin yoga, where you hold poses for longer; a brisk walk; a run without your data tracker; cycling outdoors rather than in a studio, or a wild swim; these might not kill as many cals but they are healthier choices for your mind and body in the long term. And don't forget being still is as important as moving for mastering solitude.

And it's this attitude I've tried to apply to my eating as well. Food should be enjoyed. There is nothing less joyful than being the person at the table who, and not because of any medical condition, orders a drab salad with dressing on the side while everyone else tucks into an abundant meal with gusto. Balance and careful moderation are a gentlewoman's middle names and while it is smart to self-regulate and think, 'OK, as I treated myself to a cheese course and pudding yesterday, I will enjoy a lighter meal today', it's important to be aware that self-regulation can quickly turn into self- flagellation.

Gentlewomen treat themselves how they'd treat others. You'd never tell anyone else they were lazy for not making a 7am gym class, or fat for ordering chips on the side, so why would you say such things to yourself? Eating well and exercising are opportunities to spend some good, meaningful time getting to know yourself; they are not punishments.

I realize carving out time for yourself when others rely on you can feel like an impossible privilege, but it is necessary, and it doesn't need to involve leaving the house: you can simply have a bath instead of a quick shower, or go to bed 30 minutes earlier than usual to read a book. Me time can be a cup of tea in the garden before anyone else in the house wakes up, or walking to the office. The challenge is to take these breaks consistently, particularly if you have children or someone else who needs looking after, but these don't need to be long stints – even 20 minutes can make a difference and help you find your own balance and rhythm.

Truly befriending yourself, like any relationship, takes time and effort. You need to be with yourself in different kinds of situations so you can engage with how you react in them, challenge yourself and learn something new about the kind of person you can be.

If the thought of a solo excursion fills you with dread, here is a simple guide to how you might approach it:

STEP ONE: SWIPE RIGHT ON YOURSELF

Start by taking yourself on a date to figure out how you feel about your own company. But keep it casual just in case you're not as attractive or charming as you thought. Book a cinema ticket in advance so you can't change your mind at the last minute. Choose a seat at the end of a row so you're less self-conscious. Order all the non-crunchy snacks you want and a mini bottle of wine. Enjoy not having to share.

STEP TWO: BREAKFAST CLUB OF ONE

The long-term aim is to be able to enjoy leisurely dinners on your own but let's start with the least intimidating meal of the day. Take yourself out for coffee and a croissant, read the papers or a book. You deserve to make that latte last at least another hour.

STEP THREE: NOW WE'RE COURTING

Time to make a bit more effort. Plan a special day out for yourself. Go to a gallery or museum; take a boat ride or a long walk. Graduate to lunch alone but don't grab a sandwich because 'it's just me so what's the point'. The point is to be as kind to yourself as if you were with company. If you were trying to impress someone where would you go? Go there. Always have a book or notebook in your bag and instead of gabbing with a friend or grabbing your phone, read, think and jot down your musings.

STEP FOUR: MAKE OR BREAK

This is a big step and it isn't easy. Go to a party without a plus one. Best case scenario it's full of people you know and you are quickly swept up in their company. Worst case, you're on your own. Walk confidently into the middle of the room – avoid the periphery and don't chicken out and start playing with your phone. Look up, shoulders back, eye contact, smile. Make an effort to introduce yourself and talk to at least three people. The minimum time you should stay is as long as it takes you to finish a first drink. The great thing about being alone is being able to do what the heck you like without thinking of anyone else, so if you aren't having fun, leave, but leave with your head held high because you did it. This takes guts, which indicates you are starting to implicitly trust yourself more and more.

NB: when you feel as though everyone is watching and judging you, they are not, you are.

STEP FIVE: SINGLE ROOM PLEASE

Go on holiday or at least a trip alone. In some ways this is easier than step four as you can be as unsociable as you like. The challenge here is not driving yourself to absolute distraction and feeling lost in your loneliness. A short break alone is a great test of confidence in your own company but don't overestimate how interesting you are. Pack or download enough books and podcasts and sign up for activities. I suggest starting with no more than three nights away on your own. After this time, you may find yourself wanting to send *yourself* a break-up text explaining, 'It's not you, it's me…or is it both of us?'

I'm not glorifying loneliness, as too much time spent with only the incessant rattle of your interior monologue for company can lead to completely losing perspective and becoming so withdrawn you forget how to engage confidently with another person. Indeed, small issues become magnified as they turn over and over in your mind and you become hyper-sensitive to the slightest form of rejection as your solitariness intensifies into unlearning socialization. Learn to recognize this in yourself and make the first move before such feelings overwhelm you. It's easy when you're a bit low or vulnerable to begin your story with 'no one ever invites me out', 'my friends never text me', 'no one cares about me'.

Part of being a gentlewoman is accepting that often if you don't initiate plans, no one else will. This isn't because you have bad friends who don't want to see you, but people are consumed with being the protagonists in their own narratives, so they need a little prompting and that is a gentlewoman's duty. Remember, they might not realize that you're feeling down or hard done by or lonely unless you tell them. Don't be a victim. Be the agent of your own happiness. Send a text or two, be honest about needing company, make a plan and make it happen.

Olivia Laing writes:

> *So much of the pain of loneliness is to do with concealment, with feeling compelled to hide vulnerability, to tuck ugliness away, to cover up scars as if they are literally repulsive. But why hide? What's so shameful about wanting, about desire, about having failed to achieve satisfaction, about experiencing unhappiness?*[1]

It's easy to feel like you're never alone with a smartphone – the whole world is in the palm of your hand. But what are you left with when the battery runs out? Who are you when you aren't sharing your world? One of my favourite ever *New Yorker* cartoons depicts a woman crossing a finish line between two trees and the caption asks whether she actually ran a marathon through a forest, if social media didnt upload and share it.

A gentlewoman must never mistake followers and likes for the real thing: real friends and real love or validation. In today's world of instant gratification, where you barely have to think about needing something before it's dropped by drone onto your doorstep, we are losing the ability to wait, to be bored, to be alone or sit by ourselves. Every second of our day is consumed by images, messages, opinions and facts and perhaps it's only by powering off our devices that we can truly connect with our authentic selves.

During this process of self-discovery, I found out that I spent a disproportionate amount of time thinking about reality television characters, could not iron a shirt well, had a surprising penchant for the music of Korean boy bands and was misusing the term 'several' to mean roughly seven of something rather than three or more. I also spent enough time alone with my thoughts at that particular juncture of my life to decide that despite finding out my dad was leaving my mum for a much younger woman, my view of him as a father could be different to her opinion of him as a husband. Although my parents' separation meant I had my own issues with my dad, I didn't have to feel guilty for not hating him.

Spending a good amount of time alone gives you the space to contemplate how you feel, away from other people's expectations and unclouded by their emotions and individual experiences. So whatever it is you may be grappling with that has affected you in a way that may be different from the way it has affected other people you are close to, take the time to contemplate this without their distraction. It's important to listen to other people's stories and respect their views but you don't have to take them on as your own. Gentlewomen must consider this on a wider, less personal scale too, in an age when mass outpouring of feeling is easier to access than ever, to the extent that we can voyeuristically peer into one billion Instagram users' lives by searching through their emotional hashtags #blessed #emo #ptsd #excited #lifegoals et al.

The more you know yourself, why you do the things you do, why you react in the way you do and what provokes an emotional outpouring or stoical resolve, the easier it is to be kinder to yourself. And once you're truly kind, understanding and compassionate with yourself, you'll find it easier to be the same with others. So get a date in the diary now for some quality time, because in the words of RuPaul Charles: 'If you don't love yourself how the hell are you gonna love somebody else?'[5]

Gentle suggestions for being alone

- If dining alone, it's best to sit up at the bar, if there is one. Take a book, magazine or newspaper for company.
- Walk there if you can.
- Wake up early or stay up late and make one of these times sacred and just for you.
- If drinking alone at home, avoid wine as there's a danger you'll finish the bottle. Fix yourself an Old Pal (see page 72). Savour every sip.
- Exercise is best enjoyed without a fitness tracker.
- Keep a notebook and pen with you at all times.
- Remember: two episodes of your favourite show in one sitting is always enough. Delayed gratification is more satisfying than bingeing.
- Cook nice food for yourself, not worrying about the calorific content, and lay the table, pour yourself a drink; hell, put lemon in your water, you deserve it.
- Never ever waste time alone by staring at your phone – you will never get that time back.
- Take yourself on a date once a month – go to the cinema, a gallery, or catch a play at the theatre.
- Read the papers in public on a Sunday.
- Find spots that accommodate your *sans* plus-one dates.

CHAPTER 4

Being sociable

There's a moment, before the first party guest rings the doorbell, when your home seems heavy with the weight of possibility. How will the night go? Your living room – crisps, nuts and olives in bowls, cushions plumped – is holding its breath. Wine glasses stand to attention on the counter, and bottles are lined up, ready for action. You swish on lipstick, hide your slippers under the bed. And then... It all happens at once: people arrive bearing booze, you're given six bunches of gladioli and there aren't enough vases, someone turns up with a pineapple, the playlist is on, corks are popping, you're being hugged and kissed by every arrival. Then suddenly you're dancing, you're insisting everyone does shots, you're outside with the smokers wearing someone else's coat. And before you have a chance to think 'Hey, I'm hosting a really good party,' everyone has left (apart from that one person asleep on your sofa). The bottles are empty and the only sound is the ping of WhatsApps, saying: 'Home safe, thanks for a great night (dancing girl emoji).'

Gentlewomen are the hosts with the most.

But you don't need a big home or a big budget – just a bit of imagination and careful planning.

STEP ONE: A GOOD PARTY NEEDS A *RAISON D'ÊTRE*

What are you celebrating and why? Birthdays, Christmas, New Year's Eve, engagements – all such events come laden with tradition and predictability. But if your celebration is something unique, then no one knows what to expect and you can surprise and delight your guests, free from any preconceived notions. Here are some events you may want to consider celebrating in future:

Mercury is in retrograde;

You quit your job;

You started a job;

It's the last episode of your favourite TV show;

You're single again;

Beyoncé just dropped a surprise album;

The clocks went back/forward;

You got a pet;

Solstice;

Tuesday.

STEP TWO: GET PREPPY

Good hosting is 80 per cent what happens before your guests arrive, 20 per cent what happens on the night. If the spirit of Dionysus spontaneously moves you to think hosting a party is a good idea, give it 24 hours before you send out invites. Check your schedule, check with whoever you share your home or life with and pre-check that at least two of your favourite people can be there to support.

Once you've decided on your party's purpose, a gentlewomanly approach is to let it subtly inform the mood of the event – perhaps serve a cocktail in its honour – rather than let it become a full *mise en scène*. When hosting, if you want your guests' attire to nod to your party's theme, make a suggestion such as 'wear yellow', which allows for various degrees of interpretation but is clearly not an opportunity to come as a banana.

You'll need enough glasses (and spares in case more people turn up or any get broken) – proper glasses. Nothing tastes good in a plastic cup and the oceans will not thank you for such non-recyclable waste. So stock up on scores of cheap wine glasses and champagne flutes for such occasions.

Plan to serve food at at least two junctures throughout the night. Canapés make a good impression. Serve something simple (and not time-consuming) such as bread and cheese at around 8/9.30pm and have something to offer your last guests before they head home – falafels and hummus make a classy equivalent to a late-night kebab.

Yes, we canapé!

Buy a few packs of medium-sized crostini or blinis. Spread some with olive tapenade and some with cream cheese (with grating of lemon zest) and top with a small slice of cornichon or smoked salmon (caviar optional). Serve them on big plates and ask your best-looking male friend to offer them around to guests. Do give cocktail napkins out too – no one wants sticky fingers.

Serving food stops people from getting too wasted, and as the host you want your guests, and yourself, to maintain a merry level of merry and not veer into weird or sabotage-territory drunk, because it only takes one lairy bore, who perhaps was at the pub before your party, to make everyone self-conscious. Have big jugs of ice water on hand and make sure you drink one soft drink for every alcoholic one – at the *very* least for the first few hours of the party.

The best guests will bring a contribution but running out of booze is nothing short of a catastrophe, so do the math and make sure you can provide for the number of people invited. If it's getting too expensive then downsize. It's cute to be able to offer a few simple cocktails but seriously, keep them simple: you need to be able to enjoy your party as much as you want everyone else to. If you are in the kitchen fiddling with Angostura bitters and an uncooperative pipette all night you're no good to anyone. Mix up jugs of easy cocktails in advance and delegate to one of your most trusted friends the task of keeping them topped up.

STEP THREE: IN THE MOMENT

In fact, it's a good idea to enlist a co-host for the night so while one of you is doing the hosty housekeeping – taking coats, serving drinks, laying out food – the other is circulating, aka breaking people in.

People always gravitate towards and then congregate in the kitchen at house parties, prepare for this – keep the surfaces clear, put glasses and beverages where people can find them and remove anything precious. If people bring food, decant things into bowls and put flowers in vases or else a mess of plastic bags and pots of guacamole will quickly mount up. Stealthily keep on top of cleaning up. In between chatting to people quickly and quietly swoop through the house getting rid of rubbish. Nothing says 'after party' like empty packets of crisps and half-eaten tubs of salsa.

Put some thought into lighting so that your guests will look their best and your home will take on a sexy new nocturnal personality. Light candles (not tealights, which burn out quickly and look sad) and dim the overhead lights gradually as the night progresses. Having a scented candle in the bathroom is a nice but not necessary touch.

Build a playlist in advance. Don't let anyone else take over the music – there's always someone at a party who thinks their taste in tunes is better than yours and is desperate to be DJ. But as soon as you let someone play 'just this one song' it's not long before someone else has 'just this one track' they have to hear *right now*, and before you know it the party totally loses its flow. And speaking from personal experience, for goodness' sake don't just hit shuffle on your iTunes and hope for the best: nothing kills a dance party like your *Hypnobirthing* audiobook suddenly playing at full blast.

How to perfect a party playlist

Clara Amfo is a TV presenter and DJ on BBC Radio One.

How do you set the mood of your party with music from the minute people walk through the door?

Start with a really familiar record that everyone knows and loves. When it was my house-warming, I put on *The Miseducation of Lauryn Hill*. For me, that album is just like a warm hug. Choose something that all your friends grew up loving, rather than going straight in with the current massive bangers – save them for later. You want to kick off a house party with something familiar and comforting.

HOW TO BE A GENTLEWOMAN

How do you play tracks so they build with the flow of the party?

Think about a song, whether it is current or classic, that you know
is going to make your friends scream, like, 'Oh my God, this is my
song!' Everyone has got that tune. And work your way up to that
being a 'moment' with your playlist. Let's say your party starts at
9pm. People are not going to start getting there until about 11pm,
so I would want to play that song around midnight – everyone's
loose, everyone is bedded in, and they are committed to dancing.
Often at parties people can be a little bit shy and won't start
dancing straight away. With me and my friends, for example, if
someone plays, 'It's Not Right But It's Okay' by Whitney Houston,
I know for a fact that I will see at least two or three of my friends
lip-syncing to it, and everyone has just become super excited. I
think iconic songs like that are really useful for those moments.

**Do you think that there should be some kind of consistency
to playlists?**

No, go eclectic all the way. At the best parties you could be
dancing to house one minute, disco the next, then grime,
bashment, boogie, funk, a random David Bowie song in the mix
– it doesn't matter! If people are committed to having a good
time, they will follow you on that musical journey. I love a playlist
that isn't afraid to show people who you are, because you have
the intuition to play, for instance, obscure French rap, but then
chuck in a Mariah Carey deep cut, just because you can. I like
fearlessness in a playlist. Of course, there has got to be a level
of safety there, songs that everybody knows and that make
people feel good, but I like playlists to take risks.

———————————————————————————

STEP FOUR: GET THE GUEST LIST RIGHT

The best parties comprise enough people who already know each other, but not so many that it becomes cliquey. Diversity is key for interested people and interesting conversations – a mix of friends from all parts of your life, who maybe have very different jobs, outlooks and styles but have you in common so can enjoy getting to know each other. As the legendary doorman of Studio 54, Marc Benecke, told the BBC in an interview, 'What we really wanted was the mix.'

At the celebrated New York nightclub in the late 1970s you might have found Calvin Klein, Truman Capote, Liza Minnelli, Robert Mapplethorpe, Elizabeth Taylor and Andy Warhol partying with a classical pianist, politician or Arnold Schwarzenegger. Imagine!

Your house-party guest list may not be as stellar but an electrifying dynamic is created when you get the perfect combination of people in a room together, and that energy, which seems to come out of nowhere and blaze for a hot second then disappear in a puff of dry ice, is what makes a good party great.

A note here also about being a guest. You owe it to your host to bring your best, most charming self to the party. Turn up earlyish to make up numbers, bring bottles that aren't just for you personally to drink (even when not drinking, please), dance, speak to new people and leave like a gentlewoman.

STEP FIVE: THAT'S ALL FOLKS

Know when to call it quits. Take a look around you: has the music gone weird because someone you don't know has hopped on the Bluetooth and is playing experimental German techno? Are people slumped on sofas, not talking? At this point, you are well within your rights to turn up that dimmer switch, yawn loudly and say something along the lines of, 'I think you all live in the same direction, perhaps you could all share a cab?' That should do the job.

Knowing when to leave a party is a gentlewoman's superpower. Not only do you always have half an eye on the next day, which you will want to enjoy with your usual gusto, not waste hungover on the sofa eating takeout and blurrily staring at daytime TV, but also you are self-possessed enough to recognize when you will not have more fun than this. It's best to leave on a high. I favour a brief thanks to the host then a 'French exit' (*see* below).

Ways to leave a party

Absquatulate – to leave abruptly, perhaps in the middle of a conversation (yes, this is an actual word).

A dramatic adieu – you say goodbye loudly to everyone, thus making fellow guests feel it's time for them to leave too and inadvertently killing the party.

Electric slide – whispered thanks and side scuttle out of the door.

French exit – to slip away unseen.

'Your cab's here!' – you are politely chucked out.

I have perfected the art of absquatulating from nightclubs on the now infrequent occasions I find myself in them. The thing about clubbing is there's always that debilitating pressure to have FUN, which is second only to office Christmas parties for enforced joviality. In vast spaces with so many rooms and nooks and crannies to explore, it can be impossible to commit to staying long enough in one area to ever start enjoying it. Then we are burdened with FOMO, which means walking aimlessly from room to room feeling increasingly like an observer rather than a participator. And as we all know, when one breaks the fourth wall in a 'fun' scenario, and becomes almost frighteningly self-aware, there's no going back – if you started thinking how silly people look when dancing, you'd never dance again and that would be a shame. When you are part of a throng of revellers all of whom seem to be having a better time than you, it's useful to remember the universality of this alienating feeling. If you are ever overwhelmed in this way at a club, gig or festival, think of the individuals that comprise the mass. Most people, although perhaps not at the exact same moment as you, will have at some point or other experienced the sense of being a party voyeur. You're not alone and it's comforting to realize that however confident and cool other people seem, they too will have had moments of crippling insecurity when they became too interior or struggled to connect with a situation. A gentlewoman isn't immune to the fragility of being human, but she welcomes these shaky moments as a reminder that she is part of something bigger than herself.

The best nights out, I'm sure you'll agree, are when you are so authentically in the moment with the experience that nothing can break the spell. On those rare occasions, at a gig or a club, when you are gloriously sweaty, covered in other people's spilled drinks, completely unaware of the time or of how much your feet hurt in those shoes, but right in the centre of a crowd which is all moving to one beat and all feeling in that instant the same rush of endorphins as you, well it's addictive, even if you're stone-cold sober.

FINDING YOUR PEOPLE

When I first 'came out' at the age of 17, I was desperate to find my people. I'd got used to being on the outside, looking in. I wanted, and needed, to find where I belonged in the social world, and there was a lesbian bar in London that I was desperate to check out. It was called Candy Bar and I'd heard about it from older girls at an LGBTQ youth group I frequented in Hackney. One Saturday night in 2001, a queer school friend and I met in Soho and walked past the discreet entrance on Carlisle Street about 12 times before mustering the courage to enter. We had to sign-in, which you can imagine was a terrifying prospect for two sixth-formers on their first gay foray. My hand shook as I inscribed my name and address in the heavy leather-bound guest book, thinking this meant I was now an official lesbian – would I get some kind of certificate?

Seeing my name there at the bottom of a list of other women's gave me a first shiver of belonging. I liked being part of a special, secret club.

In gay bars I felt desired in a way I never had before, which gave me a new-found confidence and just in time. The armour I'd been wearing throughout my teenage life slipped away as I began to inhabit my true self and sexuality as a young adult.

A gentlewoman isn't afraid of feeling desired and enjoys gentle flirting with both men and women, regardless of sexual preference, because our intention isn't necessarily to get them into bed, but to make this person feel that their best self is being seen. (We should redefine 'flirting' to mean conversations that fizz with the excitement of a meaningful connection, well-placed compliments, eye contact and quick wit, not cheesy lines and innuendo.)

I experienced an ardent kind of belonging, by being part of a 'scene', and it gave me a centre of gravity at an emotionally tumultuous time. However fractured, unhappy or confused I've felt throughout my life, I've always been able to walk into an LGBTQ safe space, bar or club and feel that happy tug of togetherness.

I wonder where and how *you've* enjoyed this feeling? Think about it. In what kind of social gatherings do you feel most content, confident and relaxed? Where do you have the most fun and feel as though the other people there 'get you'? Gentlewomen make sure their evenings and weekends are comprised more of these kinds of experiences and less of everything else.

It's only really by saying yes to everything in your early twenties that you'll figure out where you feel you belong. You'll have gone to music festivals, warehouse parties, jazz bars, bashment raves, drag clubs, poetry readings, hip hop nights and everything in between. You'll have had horrible experiences when you didn't fit in, hated the vibe, couldn't stand the music and spent an inordinate amount of time hiding in the toilet. And you'll have had those truly euphoric nights when you felt changed for the better. Be clear about what, for you, constitutes a good time. And once you have put in the requisite research, trying as many different hedonistic happenings as life throws at you, you should be confident in only accepting invitations to things, or putting yourself in party scenarios, that you will most likely enjoy.

It takes emotional effort to maintain a thriving social life. Even the most extrovert among us can feel like we are going into Power Saving mode after long periods of being 'on'. Talking to people, networking, being amusing and charming, flirting – all these things can feel like hard work. It is important that you also retreat from your social life. Clear your diary for a few days and reconnect with yourself, quietly spending time alone or with your family to recharge.

But there's a marked difference between craving some alone time, being an introvert aware of her soft power, and being 'shy'. Shyness can be debilitating. As a child I couldn't bear talking to people I didn't know, I felt as if I had nothing to say. Social interactions made me anxious. I was awkwardness personified. Thank goodness for my older cousin Billie, who was naturally exuberant, charming and always knew what to say to get a laugh. She was a popular girl and I was a geek. From an early age she took me under her wing and taught me how to handle myself. Billie would talk to me, ask me questions and make me feel as though I was the most important, interesting person in the world. It took us a few years but eventually she had shone her light on me so much that I was finally able to grow, confident in my own skin. She saved me, really, from a life limited by shyness.

Not many of us start out as cool, confident and charming, and we often have a person, maybe a partner, teacher, friend or relative, who we can credit with helping us see how much easier life is and how much more fun you can have when you are confident in being yourself – however loud or quiet that self is – in social situations. It is the job of a gentlewoman to be this person for other women. If you can see that someone is struggling to connect with people or the experience at a party, shine your light on them, give them your time and your attention. You never know, such a small act of kindness could make a big impact.

My younger cousin Romy, who is now one third of the Mercury-Music Award-winning band The xx,* was even more shy than me growing up and it lasted well into her teenage years. How on earth then, you may wonder, does she overcome that natural

* Which at the time of writing has had three gold- and platinum- selling albums and performed to packed-out stadiums around the world.

setting to walk out on to Glastonbury Festival's Pyramid stage and sing to a crowd of 150,000 people? It's because she has become a gentlewoman and learned how to transform shyness – often the result of not really knowing, liking or trusting oneself – into confident quiet. I see in Romy the qualities I value most in the gentlewomen in my life. She exudes a soft power – the result of surviving hard times (the loss of both parents before the age of 21) and channelling this pain into positive creativity that inspires and uplifts others. At a party Romy will quietly listen to someone else talk or stand back while others fill the dance floor, but she has presence, and it is this that a gentlewoman, however boisterous or serious their natural way of being, should strive for.

Meet a gentlewoman

Romy Madley-Croft is one third of The xx.

As a quiet and naturally introverted person, how do you walk out on to a stage and perform to thousands of people? What switches in your head? And what can we learn from that?

I have been thinking about that a lot lately; I have been off stage for eight months now. I am getting used to being 'me' off stage and it does seem mad that I have this other life. When I am in the flow of the tour and I perform every night, it is just like jumping off a diving board. At first you think, 'I really don't want to do this.' You just stand on the edge and you think, 'What on earth is going to happen to me?' And then you do it and you're, like, 'Oh, actually that was really fun.'

So, put yourself in situations that are out of your comfort zone and just keep doing it and doing it until it feels more naturally 'you'?
Absolutely. I still have that now going into song-writing sessions with other artists, which is new for me. Meeting strangers is hard. Before I get there, I am, like, 'Actually, I can't do this. I am too scared; I am too shy to meet these people.' When I walk up to them I am really scared and I want to leave. And then I just decide, 'No, I can do this!' It is about pushing on like that.

What can people who aren't performers learn from your ability to be an introvert but still have such a presence on stage?
Well, I realized that I am not the kind of person who feels very comfortable dancing, even among my friends. So, I wasn't going to be the performer that was really moving and jumping around on stage. I had to accept that about myself. Then, observing other artists I look up to, I saw that sometimes when they stand still, and are a little bit more reserved, that's when you really take in what they are doing. So, I accepted that was my personality, and I just went with it. Now that some of our songs have got more upbeat I have found myself dancing awkwardly on stage. But it feels good, it feels kind of cathartic just to let myself go.

I think you can be at a party or a social situation and not be the most extroverted presence, but you can still be open to things and open to conversation and not stare at your feet. When I'm on stage now I try to look out at the audience, whereas before I would look at the floor and I would be too shy. So, I think that if you just look around, and you are actually there to engage, you don't have to march up to people, saying, 'Hi, what's up?' But you can look approachable in a way that is not too out of your comfort zone, to just start the conversation.

Why is it harder to be confidently yourself at a party with people you don't know than it is to sing on stage?

I think I am used to performing now. It is kind of my home to be up on stage. I have developed a sense of comfort up there where I know how *that* feels and I know how *that* looks. I would like to feel that same 'comfort' in other social situations. But I go to parties and other people seem really good at saying, '*I* did this' or 'guess what *I* did', and other people go 'wow' and they command this respect and sense of awe. I am always more than happy to be like, 'Oh, you know, I'm in a band,' but that is not something I massively crave – to really state what I have done. If people ask me questions, I do start to perk up and feel more comfortable. Essentially, though, I just enjoy listening.

Whenever I walk into a party and feel that old shyness nipping at my heels I think of Billie, holding court, a circle of people around her clutching drinks, clinging to her every word, laughing at some hilarious anecdote or another and I remember what life she could bring to an occasion by being like that – she filled rooms with infectious joy, brought people together, made them feel that they were fabulous. She was the epitome of a gentlewoman at parties and after she died I felt I owed it to her to at least try my best to keep her spirit alive in me.

I force myself to do this because there comes a time in life when shyness reads as rudeness. If you don't like talking about yourself, fine. Ask other people questions. Listening well is the most important social skill a gentlewoman can master and in this era of boundless self-expression we need more people who are truly able to exhibit empathy and give someone else the space and support they need to tell their story rather than just broadcast their own. The worst conversations are when you feel the other person is merely waiting for you to stop talking so they can begin their monologue. And as so much dialogue takes place in a digital sphere now, opportunities to connect in real-world social situations should be relished. A gentlewoman always admits when she isn't well versed in a subject and keenly learns about it from others. She is happy to lean out and understands that it is not impressive to blag your way through a conversation.

It's always a pleasure talking with someone you've only just met at a party or dinner, who makes eye contact, seems genuinely interested in you and who you feel doesn't want to be anywhere else but in conversation with you. They'll remember your name and ask meaningful follow-up questions. *Be* that person. A gentlewoman relishes the opportunity to make someone else feel good about themselves and there's nothing people enjoy more than feeling truly seen and understood even in casual social situations. I often think of this line from Simone de Beauvoir's *The Second Sex*: 'Be loved, be admired, be necessary; be somebody.'[1]

Being this person doesn't mean shouting the loudest; it means making an impact in whatever way is most true for you.

If you are someone who hates 'making small talk', then the onus is on you to elevate the conversation. You don't have to talk about your journey there, the weather or any other banal pleasantries if you don't want to.

How to work a room like a gentlewoman

- Ask 'what are you into?' not 'what do you do?'
- Always confidently outstretch an arm for a handshake rather than have to endure an awkward 'will they won't they' air kiss.
- Have an amusing anecdote up your sleeve but not one you've told a million times before or the boredom will be obvious in your voice.
- 'Will you excuse me?' is all you need to say when a conversation has run its course and you want to move on.
- Introduce people to each other and involve them in the conversation.
- When introducing yourself to strangers say your first and last name, as this instantly exudes more authority and confidence and commands respect. I've noticed men naturally do this while women will often just say, 'Hi, I'm Janet.'
- If someone is really interesting to you or seems like a useful professional contact ask for their card or have them write their details in your phone. Follow up the next morning with an email saying it was nice to meet them and you hope to keep in touch.
- Recall two or three things they have mentioned and drop them into conversation later so they feel as though you have actually listened to them.
- Use hand gestures to convey what you mean, if you feel as though your words aren't quite sufficient.
- Share something personal (but not too personal) with them so they feel as though they can trust you.

Working for well-respected magazines over the years has afforded me a place on the guest lists of London's most star-studded bashes. I've been out every night of the week at gallery openings, film premieres, shop launches, private soirées in hotel bars, gigs and Gatsbyesque wild parties. The worst were cast with posers who couldn't look you in the eye when chatting because they were constantly scanning the room in case someone more important arrived; partygoers who wouldn't commit to talking to you until they knew you were 'worth it'. For these people, being in the presence of celebrity was how they got their sense of self-worth. Such parties were cold and vacuous and I couldn't wait to leave.

How to crash a party

Jodie Harsh is a legendary drag queen, DJ and club night entrepreneur

When is it OK to crash a party?

It's OK to crash a party any time – be it a wedding, a fashion-week extravaganza or a wake. If you can offer something to the night, then you have every right to be there. If you're truly fabulous you'll gain entry and become best friends with the host by the end of the night, even if it is a dead person. And what's the worst that can happen?

What's the classiest way to blag entry?

First, pick your target – the most amenable person on the door. This could be the intern with the clipboard or the friendliest-looking security. Wait for the perfect timing and then approach the gatekeeper with utter confidence and charm, like you're just breezing in to make that party even better. We live in the social media age, so chances are you've done your research on the host or type of event prior to arrival – if you've literally just stumbled across the party then check Instagram geo-tags to see what's going on inside and who's been tagged in photos since the party started. Who's the DJ? Can you be their girlfriend? Be fearless, but never rude. Oh, and dress for the occasion – if you show up in a tracksuit it's unlikely the door host will think you're supposed to be there.

Where do you draw the line between confidence and unpleasant arrogance in such scenarios?

Politeness is always key – you don't want to appear rude or cocky at the door, because that's not the attitude of people at a good party. If you're being like that *outside* the event, the likelihood is you won't be welcomed in to behave like that inside the event.

If you're not actually on the guest list, will the way you dress help you get in?

Confidence is key – hold your head up high, walk the walk and talk the talk. Dressing the part helps, and dressing bigger than the part helps even more. You're less likely to be turned away if you look fabulous – the party needs *you* more than you need it.

TOP TIPS FOR CRASHING (AND NOT BURNING)

- Spontaneously crashed parties are always more fun than premeditated ones.
- Ask yourself how much you want to go to this party – is it worth it?

- Try to genuinely get on the guest list before blagging it – polite emails or DMs to promoters can open doors.
- Don't lie.
- State your real name clearly and confidently.
- When your name isn't on the list, don't gabble. Make eye contact, smile and say, 'Oh how peculiar, let me make a call'.
- If you haven't been let in before you step aside to make the call, it's probably best to walk away.
- Do not get drunk.
- Don't overstay your welcome.

Being in the presence of party 'rubberneckers' taught me that a true gentlewoman should treat everyone with the same degree of charm and respect. Whether they're an Oscar-winning actor or your mum's friend Margaret from up the road, you should be able to find something you can connect on. Never be snobbish about who you make the effort to be your most dashing self with and who you don't. And likewise, never be diminished by a person you might deem more glamorous or important than you.

It's easy to assume that someone we see on TV or film, or an influencer with huge social media followings, must be as confident and sorted as the personas they portray, but people in the public eye who feel under constant scrutiny often struggle with a consistent sense of themselves, as much – if not more so – than the rest of us.

HEALTHY HEDONISM

It's tempting to think that being really 'good' in one aspect of our life – as a mother, or a boss, for example – gives us licence to be 'bad' in another, as if on the scales of morality we'll still end up somewhere in the middle. But individual actions are not separate ingredients that mixed together create something so perfect you can't tell what went into it. Every single thing you do *makes* you and contributes to the whole, so if there are things about yourself you aren't proud of or patterns of behaviour that you wish you could stop, be gentle as you lean into and discover the motivating factors behind them.

There is a finite distinction that we all come up against at some point in our lives between being happily hedonistic and being unhappily out of control. The latter often comes from the liberation the former provides. As a gentlewoman you should pay no heed to peer pressure. While the people you surround yourself with should bring out the best in you and probably share your most intrinsic values, you cannot control others' behaviour. If you're in with a crowd whose approach to partying ('Shots! Shots! Shots!') differs from your own, know yourself well enough not to change in order to fit in with them. If their behaviour isn't going to affect your enjoyment of a night out, leave them to it and have a good time in your own way. You'll feel worse than you would after six Jägerbombs and a kebab if you let others persuade you into making inauthentic choices.

When someone feels pressured to keep up the performance of an idea of themselves in social contexts that they believe others have bought into, they are most at risk from the damaging effects of excess. Drugs and alcohol become the fuel that helps maintain the act, and it's not just celebrities I'm talking about here, but women like you and me who are trying to be someone they are not or attempting to feel part of something when every instinct is telling them they aren't. If you're an introvert there are so many better ways to survive a party than with Dutch courage. Engage in conversations with individuals rather than large groups and find a spot that isn't on the sidelines but where you can sit comfortably and enjoy a moment's respite from the action without closing yourself off to the possibility of talking to someone. Drinking too much or taking drugs won't solve the problem of being uncomfortable in a situation and over time will make it worse. If this resonates with you, now might be the moment to break the cycle. Drink for enjoyment but don't drink because you feel you are your better self when drunk.

Gentlewomen have put in the work to address the things about themselves that might otherwise make them reach for ways to lose control. Wanting to negate the realities of pain; a lack of confidence; not liking yourself enough to make positive choices; having things in your life you just want to stop thinking about for a night are all the wrong reasons to seek out the numbing effects of narcotics or excessive alcohol.

In his book *The Examined Life*, psychotherapist Stephen Grosz writes: 'When we succeed in feeling nothing we lose the only means we have of knowing what hurts us and why.'[2]

If you like yourself, why would you want to forget yourself? Choose to only ever put yourself in situations where you feel at your most comfortable. The slow, 'healing' process of becoming a gentlewoman will eventually help to make you feel good enough not to need a 'fun' persona. It all comes back to the central tenets of soft power: treat yourself gently when the world treats you harshly; find an antidote to the neurotic world through true meaningful connections; work because you want to fulfil your potential not fulfil society's expectations of you, and party because joy is more potent when it isn't found in a plastic baggy.

This isn't to say a gentlewoman advocates a sober life. The decision to abstain completely is a personal one, and I trust if you have made that choice it is the right thing for you. But otherwise moderation maketh the gentlewoman. In an article for the *Financial*

Times, Robin Dunbar (the 15 friends guy we discussed on page 61) charts 'humans long association with alcohol that reaches back to the mists of pre-history' and makes the case for alcohol being more valuable to our species' success than we might imagine.

> *Alcohol triggers the brain mechanism that is intimately involved in building and maintaining friendships [...] that all's-well-with-the-world effect seems to be crucial for establishing bonded relationships that allow individuals to trust each other. Drinking, seen in this light, is a profound activity. It enables humans to open up their deepest selves, giving another twist to the ancient saying, 'in vino veritas'.* [3]

Mindful drinking means...

- Being self-aware enough to know when to say 'actually I won't thanks' to the offer of just one more drink on a night out.
- Self-regulating – giving yourself a number of days off drinking in the week (at least try) or limiting the amount you consume.
- An icy glass of rosé with an *al fresco* summer lunch, a Negroni in a cut-crystal tumbler at a moody bar, a good bottle of red shared over dinner with friends. It's all about quality, not quantity.

As gentlewomen we should strive for a life in which we don't need to lose ourselves in anything or in *anyone* because we already have everything emotional and physical that we could ever need within us. It's from this position that I believe we can have the most fun and let loose without losing ourselves.

Gentle suggestions for being sociable

- Spend Sunday evening looking at your social diary for the week ahead and sharing it with your partner. If it's empty, make at least one evening plan.

- Don't agree to attend anything you know you will dread on the day – visualize the event and how you will feel as you leave your house on the way there; if it doesn't fill you with positivity politely decline with ample time before the event (see page 52).

- At a party talk to at least three new people and remember their names.

- Always make your first beverage a tall glass of water.

- Dance even if badly.

- Have a karaoke song.

- Have a signature drink.

- Don't show up at a house party empty-handed.

- Remember, nothing good ever happens after 3am.

CHAPTER 5

Being together

It was a simple beach ceremony. The bride, in a tie-dyed cotton dress, barefoot and holding what appeared to be a cheap bunch of gas-station flowers, walked to the 'altar', where in the company of a handful of close friends she looked in a mirror and declared to herself, 'I do.' This Australian woman, a life coach and self-love champion, married herself on Valentine's Day 2017, and she's not alone. In September of that same year an Italian woman invited 70 guests, bought herself a proper wedding gown and a multi-tiered wedding cake, and enlisted three bridesmaids for her self-marriage. There are even companies offering wedding planning services for sologamy (marriage by a person to oneself). 'Self-marriage gently pokes fun at a dying institution and the overwrought pretensions of modern bridal culture, while allowing women to indulge their childhood fantasies and be a princess for a day,' writes the co-founder of Marry Yourself Vancouver on her website 4everluv.com.[1] Unsurprisingly, these are not legally binding ceremonies, more rituals to promise to 'love, honour and obey my soul', as the Australian woman put it in her Instagram caption on the day along with 29 hashtags including #soulmate #powerful #ritual

#picoftheday #ido. OK, I know in Chapter 2 I encouraged you to take yourself on dates. But whoa, this escalated quickly.

Learning to show yourself the same kindness and respect you would a loved-one is a fundamental tenet of being a gentlewoman. As is enjoying your own company and not looking anywhere but inwards for a sense of completeness. These endeavours add up to a way of being that is lived quietly and consistently every day regardless of your marital status. Marrying oneself appears to me a riot of narcissism that implies we now need the institution of marriage to validate ourselves as single people, as well as when we are half of a couple.

A YouGov survey in 2018 found that just under 44 per cent of British people with a partner feel they would be useless without them. The same survey found that just a third of us (33 per cent) feel that we're only happy in a relationship.[2] In many ways there's never been a better time to be single. In a powerful essay for *New York Magazine,* 'Single Women Are Now the Most Potent Political Force in America',[3] journalist Rebecca Traister writes:

> *We are living through the invention of independent female adulthood as a norm, not an aberration, and the creation of an entirely new population: adult women who are no longer economically, socially, sexually, or reproductively dependent on or defined by the men they marry.*

Traister finds that 'In the 2012 presidential election, unmarried women drove turnout in practically every demographic, making up almost 40 per cent of the African-American population, close to 30 per cent of the Latino population, and about a third of all young voters.'

She writes:

I am not arguing that singleness is in and of itself a better or more desirable state than coupledom. Many single women, across classes and races, would like to marry – or at least form loving, reciprocal, long-term partnerships – and many of them do, partnering or cohabiting without actually marrying. Still, the rise of the single woman is an exciting turn of historical events because it entails a complete rethinking of who women are and what family is and who holds dominion within it – and outside it.

What Traister articulates so well in this piece, among other things, is the fact that being a strong, independent and entirely satisfied single person does not mean you go without that base human need for connection, which sees us seek out a significant other to share our life with. But if you are single, she argues, whether by choice or circumstance, society should put less emphasis on marriage as the end goal.

Single women are taking up space in a world that was not designed for them. They make up a new republic, a new category of citizen. If the country is to flourish, we must make room for free women, and let go of the economic and social systems built around the presumption that no woman really counts unless she is married.

If we see the institution of marriage as rooted in patriarchy then perhaps singledom, as its opposite, should be claimed as a powerfully feminine space, and rather than the tired trope of women desperate for an 'other half', we redefine the social landscape of being single so that it is seen more widely as an opportunity to make *oneself* whole. Relationships are best when two fully rounded, complete and self-sufficient individuals come together, not when two unfulfilled people attempt to fill each other's gaps. Simone de Beauvoir writes in *The Second Sex*: 'I am too intelligent, too demanding, and too resourceful for anyone to be able to take charge of me entirely. No one knows me or loves me completely. I have only myself.'[4]

Now is the time to radically rethink the narrative of your romantic life. A gentlewoman recognizes that it is all up for grabs and her life's love story doesn't need to follow any pre-existing plot. According to that same YouGov survey, people aged 18 to 24 are 69 per cent more likely to agree with the statement that marriage is outdated than those over 55, and those aged 25 to 39 are almost twice as likely (48 per cent) to think so.

If you are straight I urge you to be more gay in the way you think about your relationships and future desires. The great thing about being queer is that it provides the freedom to pick and mix traditions when it comes to how I conduct my relationships privately – gender dynamics, distribution of emotional labour, sexual proclivities, and so on – and publicly with things such as when and how we could get married and have kids.

It is this spirit of choosing for oneself that I see as vital to becoming gentlewomen, particularly in matters of the heart. Challenge yourself always, and interrogate if your actions are authentic to your personal values, not just what you think is required of you. 'Be more gay' may sound sensationalist, but what I mean is: imagine society doesn't place the same gendered expectations on the two of you in your relationship – you meet as equals – and there is no etiquette around dating or your presumed future together that you need to either adhere to or push against. What then would be possible?

Soft power is about challenging the small things. That might be who makes the first move, pays for dinner, tastes the wine, holds the door open for whom. The combined influence of these micro moments may slowly add up to long-term societal change. It's worth a try – exercise some chivalry in your romantic endeavours and see what happens. Send the first text and the follow-up one, plan surprise dates, treat them to dinner or a drink when they offer to go Dutch (if you can afford to), send them flowers, walk them to the bus stop, give compliments with confidence.

How to order wine like a gentlewoman

Ruby Smith-Merovitz is a wine expert who specializes in wine pairings and fine wine sales and trading.

What are a few good things to know about wine that mean you can choose well?

One of the beautiful things about wine is that it is ever-evolving in the bottle and from vintage to vintage, hence it's somewhat unpredictable. In order to navigate choosing wine in restaurants, shops, at parties, one needs first to understand one's own taste – or 'palate'. Make a mental note or write down wines you have enjoyed in the past (taking photos of labels can help), learn what the grape variety(ies) was and research where it was from. This may also involve a little cheeky wine tasting to further cement what you suspect your preferences are: buy a few bottles to taste or take yourself to a local dining establishment and order a few different glasses. Think about what aspects you enjoy or don't in terms of: weight, acidity, grape varieties, and some simple flavour and aroma characteristics. Knowing which grapes one prefers can be very helpful, but bear in mind the ways climate affects ripeness, as the same grapes will taste very different from different places. For example, Sauvignon Blanc tastes wildly different from Sancerre, France, than it does from Marlborough, New Zealand.

What should I bring to a date's house for dinner?
This can be a fun situation to buy wine for, as you can show a little of your own taste and put it forth as something you think your date will enjoy without too much pressure. If they are really into wine this is a good opportunity to impress by bringing something off the beaten path (with the assistance of the expertise of your local wine-shop professional). If they are not necessarily 'into wine', this can then be a good chance to bring them a style or a particular wine that you have a fondness for. If neither of the above approaches appeal to you, a moderately priced bottle of something Italian or French will typically do the trick as far as assuring quality and the desired level of 'See, I brought you something nice'.

If the waiter hands the man at the table the wine menu, what's the gentlewomanly way to respond?
First off, any respectable dining establishment should ask who will be ordering the wine before making assumptions – or simply place the wine menu on the table. Then, there should be a conversation

at the table about whether there is interest in sharing a bottle or not. If not, it's every person for themselves. If sharing a bottle is the consensus, the next phase depends on whether the gentlewoman is interested in ordering the wine. If she is not, then it should be down to whoever is – man or woman. If she is, it is perfectly polite for her to put forth that she knows a thing or two about the vine and would like to order for everyone. Personally, I like to field what the preferences or tastes at the table are, consider what people are going to eat, and make an informed decision from there.

Apparently, we are living in what has been coined 'The Sex Recession'. An article in *The Atlantic* looks at the social and technological context behind data and suggests Millennials are 'launching their sex lives later and having sex less frequently than previous generations'. [5] Journalist Kate Julian interviewed a cross-section of young Americans for the piece, many of whom described 'an emerging cultural reality' in which, as one of her interviewees put it, 'no one approaches anyone in public any more'. And the data backs this up. A 2017 YouGov / *Economist* poll cited by Julian found 17 per cent of Americans now aged 18–29 believe that a man inviting a woman out for a drink 'always' or 'usually' constitutes sexual harassment.

In previous chapters we've looked at the importance of taking yourself on dates and of treating your friends as you might a new lover and planning 'dates' with them too. So when it comes to romantic 'courting', a gentlewoman should be in her element. She will take a flirtation offline as soon as possible and agree to meet in person, perhaps even – brace yourself – speaking on the telephone first. It is indeed a 'miserable impasse' if human connection exists most fully in a virtual world of right swipes and double taps. Because nothing can replace the unexpected joy of meeting someone for the first time and experiencing the visceral rush of attraction. As you lock eyes an electric current passes between you that says, 'I know that you know that I know I'm into you', and that moment has the power to make you feel alive in a way no aubergine emoji ever could. I'm not suggesting a gentlewoman should never search for love online, but she should be equally bold when there isn't a screen between herself and her desires.

At this moment in history, women have the unique power to re-address the dynamics of dating. Good men are quite rightly leaning out after the '#metoo' revolution, and thinking twice about consent and their romantic approach, but there is still space for us to playfully and respectfully write our phone numbers on napkins, strike up conversations with good-looking strangers, be confident, and slide out of Instagram DMs into real-world flirtation like never before.

We can apply our soft power to help shape what we want from a man (if that way inclined). Behaving like the strong, confident, charming woman you are on a first date – leading the conversation, ordering the wine – will surely sort the wheat from the proverbial man chaff. The kind of man threatened or discombobulated by a gentlewoman is sadly not the Darcy to her Elizabeth or the John Legend to her Chrissy Teigen.

Types of person beginning with the letter 'b' that a gentlewoman has no time for

- Bad boy wannabes.
- Bad dressers.
- Bangers on.
- Banter-fuelled lads aka basic blokes.
- Bed-making refuseniks.
- Blaggers.
- Boozers.
- Bores.
- Brutes.

Bad communication between lovers is the nexus of the plot of every work of romantic fiction for a reason. In art it makes for compelling viewing, in life not so much. If characters just said what they felt, honestly and authentically, there would be fewer misunderstandings and far less drama. While gentlewomen recognize that game-playing has a flirty frisson which can ignite a relationship in the early days, it should not be sustained after a third date. The patterns of behaviour you set up in those halcyon first few months together can define the course of your relationship should it last, so put care into the way you express yourself and your feelings from that very first text message.

It's so easy to forget to challenge embedded ways of being with a partner. When did you last really examine the distribution of chores or emotional labour? In a notebook write a list of what you give in this respect, and ask your partner to do the same. You might find it's more imbalanced than you think.

Happiness is coexisting as a couple; making an effort to still treat each other as individuals, not just fall into the matching-pyjama comfort of familiarity, through which you forget where one of you ends and the other begins. There's a reason why Kahlil Gibran's *The Prophet* is read at so many weddings:

> *Love one another, but make*
> *not a bond of love.*
> *Let it rather be a moving sea between*
> *the shores of your souls.*[6]

I believe we should exercise gentleness in the way we communicate. There should be no need to raise your voices or call each other names even if you do 'make up' after a row and you are both robust.

I ended up in a bad relationship for ten years longer than I should have been because I hadn't begun engaging with myself as a project into which I invested gentle time, thought and care to really discover and then *be* the best version of myself. The Ancient Greek poet Pindar, whose writings influenced the likes of Friedrich Nietzsche, had as the equivalent of his Tinder profile this: 'Learn and become who you are.'[7]

What better advice is there before embarking on a relationship?

A gentlewoman should embrace vulnerability because doing so can tune her in with the source of her power, but the ability to lay yourself bare, open up, admit your faults and true feelings in order to connect with yourself, and more intimately with another, is a gift that comes with experience, *after* you've done that 'learning' Pindar was on about.

We bandy around the idea of 'embracing vulnerability' these days, but we must be careful about when, how, why and with whom we do so because it is a precious thing. My friend Marissa told me about a man she dated a few years back, a pilot. He was alpha AF* she said, but he'd got into the idea of 'vulnerability' and would often send her links to articles he'd read on the subject, and one evening insisted they watch Brené Brown's TED Talk 'The Power of Vulnerability'[8] together. 'I'm naturally quite a guarded person,' Marissa told me, 'and I'd been quite aloof and deliberately distant in the first few weeks of dating as that tends to be what men find most attractive. They enjoy the chase. But this guy with all his talk of "embracing vulnerability" made me think it was OK to be a bit more honest with my feelings and let my insecurities be seen. One night in bed in a moment of low self-esteem I said to him, "You're not going to lose interest in me, are you?" And as soon as I said it I noticed a change. After that night, he waited five days before responding to a text. And then, he ghosted me. It was incredible!'

This is an example of wanting to embrace the *idea* of vulnerability as a neat 20-minute TED Talk but not as a raw, messy, challenging, unpredictable reality in a person. Don't ask for emotional truth if you can't handle the consequences of it.

Many of us are vulnerable when getting into a relationship but we don't realize it. This is when one's sense of self can be quickly subsumed and vulnerability negated by a partner's wants or needs.

* AF = as f#%k

Self-harm isn't necessarily physical. There are so many other ways that we can inflict pain on ourselves if we do not feel we are worth taking care of, and staying in a bad relationship is one of them.

It is tempting when everything else feels out of control to be able to exercise some agency over how we allow ourselves to get hurt.

Do you answer yes to any of the following questions?

1. Are you constantly scared of doing something 'wrong'?
2. Does your partner rarely ask you big questions about your values, ambitions and past experiences or even small questions about your day at work, if the niggle in your knee is better, how you're enjoying that book, etc., or actively listen and engage with your answers?
3. Do you have the same argument more than once a week?
4. Do you feel their happiness is entirely your responsibility?
5. Is there a parent–child dynamic?
6. Does discussing the future with them freak them out?
7. Do you rarely spend time with each other's friends/family?
8. Are they never the first person you call with good or bad news?

All too quickly, bad behaviours and routines become commonplace and we don't see them in their true state. They become our 'lot' and there is a vital difference between becoming subsumed by negativity and confronting it for what it is.

It's never easy to initiate a break-up, but if you are answering 'yes' to any number of the above questions and have been for a long time, it could be the only way to hold on to what makes you *you*, re-set your boundaries and allow yourself the possibility of a happy future.

When a gentlewoman splits up with a partner, she should for her own sanity and ability to move on unburdened seek to articulate her feelings to the person she is leaving or being left by. And listen to their point of view too. It might not be something you can do immediately but leave it no longer than three months before reconnecting for an emotional autopsy. Had I the resources and strength of character at the time, I would have told my ex more clearly why I believed our relationship was damaging and had to end rather than gabbling something about how desperately unhappy I was, and fleeing with nothing but my most essential possessions, never going back.

How to break up like a gentlewoman

- Give yourself time alone to really think through your feelings. Writing things down can help solidify complicated emotions. Reading books – philosophy, psychology and novels – can give you new reference points.
- Avoid talking to friends about it until you are sure(ish) in yourself about needing to break up. It's hard for other people to understand the nuances of your relationship.
- Allow your relationship every chance you can. This might mean couples therapy.
- Give your partner some warning that you aren't happy (a month for every year you've been together might be the right amount of time). It can be devastating for a break-up to

apparently come out of the blue.
- Be gentle but be clear that you want to break up, don't give false hope.
- Don't spend the night together after having your break-up conversation. You need at least a week apart to let it all sink in.
- Keep photos and mementos of your time, don't erase it.
- Don't say you want to stay friends unless you can honestly imagine a way of navigating this.

It's really hard to let go of a relationship entirely with social media at our fingertips. What Herculean resolve it takes not to just have a little look on Instagram at the Valencia-filtered tableaux of their life without you. What self-control must be exercised not to have a quick glance back through their last month's Twitter missives to see what opinions they may have developed in your absence. You can still, if you so choose, keep track of their 'online' presence in the top banner of their WhatsApp screen. And remember when Facebook was a stage for our major life moments – when changing your relationship status garnered many a 'U OK hun?', and 'it's complicated' said so much. Who to unfriend along with your ex became a Jane Austen plot in itself.

In *Existentialists and Mystics: Writings on Philosophy and Literature*, Iris Murdoch writes: 'Love is the extremely difficult realization that something other than oneself is real.'[9]

Breaking up with someone in the age of social media, having come to this 'difficult realization', involves a further emotional wrench – accepting that your ex can be 'real' and exist with someone else who isn't you. And as you're trying to recover from heartbreak, having the online version of this 'reality' just a few finger taps away doesn't help. In fact, it makes it infinitely harder.

A gentlewoman should, once having broken up 'well' with someone, avoid the urge to peek into their online world, because really, what good can come from becoming a voyeur of a world without you in it? Looking in from the outside might make you feel powerful but in actual fact it is self-sabotage.

Cue:

'Oh, so s/he has A DOG now!'

'Since when did they stay up till 4am?'

'But THEY HATE NEW YEAR'

Et al.

A gentlewoman would not do this to herself – the digital equivalent of picking at a scab. But, for me at least, it was a process of letting go, and despite how balanced and self-actualized I'd become in other aspects of my life it just took time – years, in fact – for me to stop twitching like a prettier Polonius* behind the arras.

Gentlewomen strive to maintain the powerfully feminine energy of being single when dating, dabbling, cohabiting or marrying. Because if you still have your patriarchal hegemony glasses on when you start seeing someone new (you know the big square ones with ultra thick lenses and masking tape holding the frame together at the nose) it's easy to view a traditional, heteronormative trajectory as your only option. But true love doesn't follow a linear course and nor should you – you'll end up a passenger on a runaway train hurtling towards those make-or-break life decisions (get married, break-up, have kids?). Better to be

* A character in Shakespeare's *Hamlet*, whose suspicious nature leads to him being unintentionally stabbed to death as he hides behind a curtain (arras) spying on Hamlet.

the ringmaster of your love life, in the middle of the wild, sprawling action, exercising a healthy degree of control as it plays out.

Having to be on guard all the time, ready to defend yourself or reprimand your partner, is not an environment a gentlewoman or a healthy relationship can thrive in. If you operate from a place of constant exasperation with your partner, where you are just waiting for the next thing to be annoyed about, or the next row to blow up and blow over, you are depleting your valuable – and they are so valuable – energy reserves on negativity. Fighting is exhausting and unnecessary. I'd urge you to really ask what you are gaining from this life with each other.

Perhaps you feel it is better to stay together, even if the thing created when you add yourself to your partner is now nasty, difficult, unkind or not the sum of who you are as individuals any more. If something is not good for you, as a gentlewoman you should realize that it also isn't good for the people who rely on you.

Rather than let an issue fester and tell yourself that an abstract notion of 'family' or 'love' is all you need even when you don't appear to 'like' each other very much at all, face into the reason your relationship is coming apart. A gentlewoman will of course try everything in her arsenal to make it work, but there comes a time, and you will know it, when staying with the wrong person has eroded your sense of self, your joy and your future so completely that there is nothing but dust. Take action to protect yourself, and those who need you to be at your best, and be brave enough to initiate a break-up.

However bad a relationship has been, it will have taught you something important about yourself and what you want from a future partner or from a single life. Figure out what this is and settle for nothing less. Be grateful for your ex...Thank you, next.

Gentle suggestions for being together

- Send the first message.
- Learn about wine but don't be a bore.
- Never lie. Even about small things.
- You don't need an excuse to send flowers.
- Listen as much as you talk.
- Go on long walks with your lover.
- Buy them books.
- Don't snog in public. Hand holding and a spontaneous kiss is fine.
- Never get a tattoo to mark a relationship.
- Talk about the future.
- Limit TV dinners to once or twice a week.

CHAPTER 6

Being at work

A gentlewoman never has lunch at her desk. Doing so demonstrates a lack of imagination and means you have succumbed to the 'done thing' in the office or let your workload take precedence over your quality of life. Even if you are eating a Tupperware full of last night's leftovers to save money, there's always somewhere else you can sit and enjoy it that isn't facing your computer. You might think it doesn't matter – you want to scoff a Pret sandwich with one hand and keep working or doing some online shopping with the other, but it matters greatly because it suggests you don't respect yourself and your allotted personal time enough to do something better with it. And are you seriously at peace with getting cheese and pickle stains on your mouse mat or bits of quinoa stuck in the keys of your laptop?

I've worked in offices for years and I'm always shocked by how few people take a lunch break. A study by Total Jobs found that a third of UK employees never leave their workplace after they arrive in the morning. More than half of the 7,135 people surveyed don't take their full lunch break; 68 per cent justified skipping lunch by saying they had too much to do or an unexpected task to handle.[1]

It takes, what, ten minutes to eat lunch if you are on a pressing deadline – is it *really* impossible for you to sit somewhere else in the office or dash downstairs to a nearby bench? If you are giving eight or more hours of your day to work, whether it's for a company or for yourself, you deserve to claim a small amount of time within those hours to do something completely different. So be a gentlewoman and use your time wisely and actively.

I appreciate that eating lunch in a restaurant or café might be prohibitively expensive, but if you can afford to treat yourself once a week, once a month even, to a proper sit-down lunch, alone or with colleagues, you will realize how such an enjoyable and civilized experience can break the monotony of the working day and mean you return to your tasks with renewed energy and a clarity of mind.

A gentlewoman's lunch break

- Take an actual newspaper or magazine (not an app on your smartphone) to read at a café.
- Eat a healthy, filling lunch. Finish with a coffee or herbal tea.
- Be a flâneuse (a female flâneur) and go for a gentle walk – find a river or a park ideally but an amble through city streets will do – and take in your surroundings: look up, look around, notice people.
- Exercise – go for a run (as long as there are showers in the office) or take a city bike and go for a ride; go to the gym if you're a member and finish with a quick blast in the sauna or steam room if there is one.

- Write a postcard to someone to say you're thinking of them.
- Visit a museum and have a quick look around the free permanent collections.
- Phone someone you haven't been in touch with for a while – walk and talk.
- Find a spot to sit down in with a notebook and write a list of things on your mind.
- Listen to an album you've never heard in full before.
- Arrange a power lunch with someone you want to connect with professionally.
- Meet a friend or family member at their place of work for a change.

Taking a 'power hour' every day stops you from losing sight of yourself during the working week and becoming entirely subsumed by a 'job'. When you are in the zone it's easy to forget that you exist as a person beyond that spreadsheet or keynote presentation or the 500-word article you have to write by 4pm… But your output will be better if you give yourself space and keep a healthy check on the impact work makes on the scales of your life. We strive for equilibrium, but the idea of a work / life balance feels out of step with the way we work today. There is no forward slash – life is in work and work is in life and it's all one big melting pot of experiences, which we as gentlewomen and authors of our own narrative, captains of our own happiness, exercise complete control over. And just as being stuck in a bad relationship can hold you back from becoming your full self, so can being unhappy at work.

Meet a gentlewoman

Samantha Clarke is a happiness consultant, career coach and founder of the Growth & Happiness School.

How do you know if you are unhappy at work?

If any of the following points resonate strongly with you, then there is a pretty good chance it's time to reassess your job:

— Are you anxious, unable to sleep, stressed?

— Do you fear interactions with certain co-workers or your boss?

— Do you disagree with company values or its mission?

— Do you dislike the product or service you are selling/creating/ developing?

What can you learn from being in a job you don't enjoy that can have a positive influence on your future career?

Resilience, persistence, a way to smooth out the kinks in your interpersonal skills, the ability to bolster strengths that you might be under-using and strengthen transferable skills. Often we forget about the networks and contacts we build too. Plus it's important to identify what this job is doing for you/what positive purpose it is serving you. Is it:

— your bread and butter as part of your portfolio career revenue streams?

— the manageable job you can do while you continue learning a new skill/build up customers for a new product or service?

— a job you need to stay in for a set amount of time while you pay off debt or while your partner irons out a new freelance gig or new business idea?

— an escape from your toxic previous job, giving you some
breathing space while you think about your future career?

When do you know it is time to move on?

I always advise my clients that sitting in the messy bit for a while
and taking stock of where the pros and cons are ensures you will
make considered moves. Obviously a job *you don't enjoy* is very
different to *one that is damaging your health or super toxic*. But all
too often we can be too quick to run from our emotions, concerns
or issues with one job because 'we don't like it' into the mire of
another that looks glossy from the outside. Weigh up the pros and
cons and keep your eye on the job market. If you are certain it is
your job, not another aspect of your life, that is the problem, making
sure you are fully prepared for the next move should mean you are
less likely to have a knee-jerk reaction and find yourself in a similar
position another six months down the line.

If you don't take gentle care of yourself in the ways we've
discussed in previous chapters, it's not just the pressure to
perform well or succeed at work that can feel stressful. The most
future-facing companies recognize that showing up at an office
at a certain time every day can be seriously exhausting in itself
and they've done away with the nine-to-five so that the working
day can be structured to fit around individuals. Flexible working
or self-employment suits a gentlewoman's desire to show up fully
in every aspect of her life and create an everyday 'flow' in which
she controls her own orbit of work, family, friends, relationship,
home and time for herself. If working freelance is not an option

for you, speaking to your boss about flexible hours should be. Be the change you want to see happen.

We often don't allow ourselves enough sleep, waking early after a late night seeing friends or family or staying up to watch the Netflix show everyone's talking about, in order to rush into work as if someone is taking a register at 9am. Over time the effect of this is draining. Being late is a bad habit so if a start time isn't working for you and people are keeping track, have an honest conversation about a more fluid approach to your hours, rather than feeling 'behind' before you've even reached the office. Given that most of us check our work emails as soon as we wake up, the idea of work having a 'start time' is pretty redundant anyway.

If you are in a position to exercise some agency over how much sleep you get each night, make the most of it. Stagger your week so that you avoid consecutive late nights. Choose to watch a 30-minute show rather than one that lasts an hour and if it's already 9pm by the time you sit down to press play, perhaps consider having a bath and getting into bed instead. When we are tired at the end of a long day we often don't make the best choices – from what to eat for dinner (takeout?) to how to spend those precious hours between getting home and going to bed (mindlessly scroll through Instagram? Put unaffordable clothes on wish list? Read about celebrity flaunting cleavage instead of reading pile of books on bedside table? Think about sorting underwear drawer?). If in doubt, prioritize a good night's sleep over everything else. As Homer writes in *The Odyssey*: 'There is a time for many words, and there is also a time for sleep.'[2]

A gentlewoman prefers to eat breakfast at home before bracing herself for work. It's trendy to make fussy Instagramable smoothies and acai bowls, but I feel that two slices of thick brown toast with butter and marmite or jam is no bad way to start the day (obviously this is by no means draconian – begin the day how you want to begin it!). Don't heap pressure on yourself to have a hipster healthy avocado-based morning feast or a post-gym smoothie, because before you've even left the house you are drawing on your energy reserves by having to perform what you think you ought to be doing rather than trusting your instincts.

I've commuted to offices from various homes on the outskirts of the city all my professional life. My longest journey was a 15-minute walk to the station followed by an hour standing on a packed train. I'd arrive exhausted, having pushed and bashed and shouldered my way through the crowds. I'd secretly compete with other commuters, racing particular people down tunnels as we charged through the line interchange at stations. If someone was slow or dared to stand on the wrong side of the escalator I'd be exasperated and say loudly, 'EXCUSE ME PLEASE!' I'd squeeze myself on to packed carriages rather than wait three minutes for the next train and stand with my face in someone's armpit trying not to feel desperately depressed. It was me versus everyone else, a fight that I had to win, or at least survive, and doing this in the rush hour, in both directions, five days a week, had my cortisol levels running at 'Double Espresso'.

Such a journey is common in any big city and we've come to accept that this is just part of 'going to work'.

It was while waiting for Oxford Circus station to reopen after overcrowding one night, in a throng of angry people all wielding big black umbrellas against the freezing drizzle like battle shields, that I thought, *Why am I doing this to myself?* I went and sat in a nearby bar, ordered an Old Pal and contemplated my aggressive attitude to commuting. It had to stop because my health and happiness were suffering. I needed to take back control and put some joy and kindness into the grey reality of traversing my city. The fact was I had to travel from the very east of London to the very west every day. I was working in a senior role on a weekly magazine and as it went to press every Monday I had to be in the office before 9.30am each morning for us to have any chance of meeting that deadline. I needed to make this daily public-transport trek to the office less bad for myself.

Rather than seeing my fellow passengers as being in the way, I decided to pay more attention to them as people with interesting places to go and stories to tell. Instead of refusing eye contact and staring at my phone I started looking around me. Suddenly I was smiling, offering my seat to people, letting them in front of me, holding lift doors open for them rather than willing them to close before they could get in. I'd help people carry buggies and suitcases up stairs, I'd ask lost-looking tourists if they needed help with directions and I began to say good morning to the people I'd see on the platform of my local station every day. Mindful commuting takes the anger out of the experience and I'd arrive at work in a far better mood than when I approached it like having to complete the final level of a video game.

Powering, head down, from home to the office and vice versa contributes to the very real Rushing Woman's Syndrome[*] that is endemic in our urban working lives. I've talked about how when we aren't 'rooted' or are experiencing a lack of connection with ourselves, 'busyness' can become a badge of honour. At work this can manifest itself in choosing to take on more than you need to

---

[*] Australian nutritional biochemist Dr Libby Weaver coined the term in a book of the same name published in the UK in 2017. In it she analysed the impact that a constant state of rushing has on women's health and the biochemical effects of always being in a hurry. 'You might not think you're particularly harried, but your liver, gall bladder, kidneys, adrenal glands, thyroid, ovaries, uterus, brain and digestive system certainly do,' she wrote.[3]

in order to experience the validation that 'having so much to do' affords, (*see aforementioned* eating lunch at desk).

Staying in the office late when it isn't necessary is another way those afflicted with Rushing Woman's Syndrome can fill up the spaces in their lives with the wrong thing. Having to rush home or out for drinks with friends, or to the cinema on a second date – always running just late enough to feel important and 'needed' elsewhere – is a waste of a gentlewoman's energy. Instead, know when to take your foot off the gas and make an effort to snatch pockets of time for yourself however you can.

If your contracted hours end at 5.30, leave the office at 5.30 and if you don't want to go straight home and switch straight into family mode, go for a quiet gin and tonic (or herbal tea) on your own before making the journey. Take a walk, do some exercise, run a bath, do anything before going out socially that isn't just staying at work. Every minute counts, so own your time and make it matter. But how do you know, particularly if you are new to a job or junior and trying to make a good impression, when you do need to stay late and when doing so is unnecessary?

Stay

Is there something important happening the next morning that you need to prepare for tonight? *Work quickly and efficiently to get it done.*

Is there a reason you can't complete the tasks at home? *Do what you need to do in the office and finish it at home.*

Are the rest of your team staying? *Be a team player but if you're not adding any value don't just stay for the sake of it. Ensure there's actually something to do.*

Is there a hard deadline that means you have to get your bit done not to hold up other people? *In this instance leaving a job unfinished would be selfish.*

Were you aware in advance that this would be a late night and were you given enough notice to plan your life accordingly? *This is good management. Respect it.*

Go

Do you like to clear your inbox at the end of every day? *Unnecessary! Do it on the way home or into work the next morning.*

Are you just really into something and you don't want to break the flow? *Good for you but being over-tired and working longer than you need to in a day will have a damaging effect on your flow in the long run.*

Do you think your boss will be impressed when she finds out you're still in the office at 10pm? *I have been this boss and the answer is no. It makes me think you can't manage your workload or are inefficient.*

Is the office more comfortable than your home? *See Chapter 1.*

Do you just have a vague sense of wanting to be ahead or on top of things? *Rest, sleep and socializing will be far more beneficial.*

Being a martyr, thriving on stress and exhaustion and staying in the office late or at weekends when you don't have to are signs that you are out of balance and taking your sense of worth from work (note the '*have*' to – there are obviously certain professions in which unsociable hours are imperative), rather than from having worked on yourself.

A gentlewoman needs to give a lot of herself to feel calm, confident and in control when working with a team. She is a solver of problems, a putter of things into perspective, a champion of fairness and kindness, who isn't afraid to indulge her playful spirit and sense of humour however senior she becomes. Because levity and an ability to laugh at oneself can lift the mood of an office and the morale of a team.

There's a difference, though, between confidence and arrogance – confidence takes a seat at the table, arrogance puts its feet *on* the table. When I pivoted industry, moving from a 15-year career as a magazine journalist and editor to a role as a creative director in a big advertising agency, I was rather horrified, walking through the swanky open-plan offices, to note the number of my colleagues who sat with their feet on the desks. *How unhygienic*, was my first thought – given that these are the same people who then eat lunch at their desks – but also how uncouth. In one of my initial meetings at this agency I sat next to another creative director who positioned himself so that not only were his feet up on the boardroom table but his legs were manspread as wide as possible. He placed his hands behind his head and leaned back on his chair. This was a man who was supposed to command the respect of the room, his point of view being the one that creatively shaped the project, but I couldn't take him seriously, with his Nike Huaraches in my face. What kind of ungainly power dynamic does such a stance suggest? And what entitled him to sit like he was on the sofa with a beer about to play Xbox, when everyone else in the room was sitting with laptops and notebooks, ready to work? I didn't say anything at the time (though I spent the meeting giving him my best side-eye emoji face), as I don't believe it's helpful to pull people up on behaviour in front of others, but I did send him a note after the meeting to ask politely that he never affect such body language around me again.

There are instances when it can be better to email than confront someone face to face as it gives you time to take care over how you communicate what you mean, like a gentlewoman, and them a chance to measure their response, rather than act defensively, which is the default setting when feeling attacked in person. (In fairness to this colleague, he sent a gracious apology.)

Meanwhile, during my career on staff at magazines, I once worked in an office with only one meeting room. In it was a table with space around it for far fewer chairs than there were people. This meant an unspoken hierarchy existed in the team, regarding who was important enough to take a chair and who should stand around the table. The most senior people couldn't make eye contact with the people standing behind them and there was such a stark visual indicator of who was on a different level to whom, it was impossible for everyone to feel equally valued. Then at this weekly all-team meeting I noticed a worrying trend: younger, more junior members of staff would sit on the floor. This was in a creative industry – a fashion magazine – so the office vibe was perhaps more relaxed than at, say, an investment bank. But it's not about keeping up appearances; sitting on the floor in a meeting suggests you don't care and you have nothing to input. It says, *Don't look at me, don't talk to me and don't expect me to have anything to offer this meeting*. You've demoted yourself.

We should have all stood in that meeting and got rid of the table altogether (researchers at the University of Missouri discovered that standing up for meetings can cut running time down by 34 per cent, a boon for anyone who has endured the cult of the 'pre-meeting' – a meeting about the meeting you are about to have),[4] but my colleagues shouldn't have been so quick to factor themselves out of the conversation by becoming as small as possible, sitting scrunched up on the floor like schoolkids at story-time.

My advice for women starting out in their career is: be seen. By that I mean, speak up, stand out, take initiative and listen well. In the 1861 edition of *The English Gentlewoman: A Practical Manual for Young Ladies on Their Entry into Society*, the author, who goes un-named because she's a woman so who in the 1800s cares, writes:

> *In listening, a well-bred gentlewoman will gently sympathise with the speaker; or if needs must be, differ as gently. Much character is shown in the art of listening. Some people appear to be in a violent hurry whilst another speaks; they hasten on the person who addresses them as one would urge on a horse – with incessant 'yes, yes – very good – ah!' Others sit on the full stare, eyes fixed as those of an owl, upon the speaker [...] But all these vices of manner may be avoided by a gentle attention and a certain calm dignity of manner, based upon a reflective mind and a humble spirit.*[5]

Obviously as the author is a pious woman of her times, most of her etiquette guide is vastly out of sync with life today, but some of the central tenets, such as the importance of listening well, prove perennially relevant.

An intern can be a gentlewoman and so can a CEO – people on opposite rungs of the career ladder can share a self-worth and conscientiousness that means they care about the impact they make at work, because they care about how they show up in every aspect of their lives.

A modern gentlewoman is an active member of a team. If she's in a meeting she will be fully present, ask questions and have something to contribute. She will not be on her phone answering emails, but engaging with her co-workers and contributing to the discussion, offering ideas. Maybe that means preparing a few things to say in advance, or maybe it means being brave enough to speak on the fly when something comes into your head. And if you listen well to others, you should always be able to engage and have something to add, even if it's a question, in response.

I know some people are shy (*see* Chapter 4) or anxious about saying the wrong thing or asking a stupid question, but what's the worst that can happen? A gentlewoman thinks the best of people; that they, like her, are kind, generous and keen for everyone to succeed. If you assume this of your co-workers then you'll feel comfortable and safe to be yourself around them. Of course it might not always be the case. But I'm happier if I go through life hoping that it is.

The truth is some people are the opposite of gentlewomen. They are selfish and unkind. They have a mean spirit and a twisted, negative spin on the world. It would be naive to think that everyone is your personal cheerleader, or indeed that everyone likes you at all or is interested in anyone other than themselves. There are just some bad eggs in life who will take against a gentlewoman, as she reflects back at them everything good and happy and positive that they lack. But if you expect such behaviour of other people it feeds paranoia, insecurity and instability in yourself. It also contributes to the unhelpful social narrative about women being nasty to other women professionally and not wanting them to succeed. In my personal experience, other women have been my greatest supporters far more than they have sought to bring me down.

So even if people are unpleasant, difficult or at worst bullying towards you professionally, don't let them chip away at all the good work you have done in becoming a gentlewoman. Being compassionate will help you do this. Ask why they are prone to behaving in such a way, it often means they are unhappy or have never had a good relationship with family, friends or lovers and just aren't equipped to be kind.

I learned to be my most robust and to accept fully that I couldn't make everyone like me and that that was OK during a *Devil Wears Prada* of a year at *ELLE* magazine that saw my career peak and then, well...pivot.

For two and a half joyful years I had been deputy editor to a formidable editor in chief who taught me to stick resolutely to a vision and not be afraid to ruffle feathers. I liked working for her as I felt she 'got me' and she gave me space to do things my own way, while being clear about what she expected me to deliver in return.

We were profoundly different in temperament but we complemented each other; I took on more of the pastoral care side of managing the team, having endless 'coffees' with people who wanted to talk about their role, deflecting conflict and addressing issues with workload, and she focused on the main big battles in that business, to do with the balance of commercial and creative. She had little time in between the demands of her four children, work and her steam relay swim of Lake Geneva for friendly 'catch-ups' with me or anyone else for that matter.

So when one morning I got a text message from her inviting me to meet her before work for coffee, I knew something was up. She was leaving, stepping down after 12 years at the helm of the world's biggest-selling fashion magazine for an even bigger job elsewhere. And this meant that I, her deputy, would now be the acting editor in chief of the magazine.

This was the biggest professional challenge of my life. It was my dream job, the position I'd been working towards, but was I ready for it? I didn't have much choice as the outgoing editor marched me up to the executive floor and had me sign the contract that day. I would be in charge while the role was advertised externally and a new editor in chief announced. I'd apply for the job, while doing the job...I took a deep breath and before any doubts and insecurities crept into my head I decided I could do it.

This unexpected career ascent came at the right time. I was the most stable and happy I'd ever been. If you find yourself at a professional peak, or in a challenging job at any level when you haven't got this anchoring you to what really matters, your most profound reason for being; if you don't like yourself or have faith in your true self, not just the image you can carefully curate, then such jobs can bring out the worst in you. The way you work stems from the same 'centre' of self from which comes the way you do anything, so before, or perhaps alongside, getting ahead, leaning in and smashing glass ceilings professionally, invest equal efforts personally. You will be more inspiring and effective for it.

By the time the incredible opportunity to edit *ELLE* was offered to me, I had constructed a joined-up life in which I didn't feel I had to give less of myself to anyone or in any situation. If I was ever, personally, going to be in the right place to take on such a big role – keeping the business of a fashion magazine running and creatively thriving; managing a team of brilliant, complex people, all experts and artists in their field, while putting together the job application of a lifetime, knowing that fashion and media doyennes from around the world would be after it too, some willing me to fail – well, that time was now.

All industries have their own 'scene', complete with gossip and scandal, a cast of starring and supporting roles, various dramas, occasional tragedies and constant twists and turns. The world of fashion magazines is no exception. There was much speculation among colleagues on other publications and my own as to who would get the job. 'Have you heard so-and-so has applied?', was a near-constant refrain. It was hard, knowing all eyes were on me and how *ELLE* looked under my leadership, to stay calm and measured during the months that I ran the magazine while waiting to find out if I'd be able to claim the job of editor as my own. This is what worked for me:

A gentlewoman's guide to keeping work in perspective

- Take time each day to do something totally unconnected to your day job.
- Don't get drawn in to moaning and encourage others to try to change something they are not happy about rather than revel in complaining about it.
- Talk to friends in other industries and get their perspective.
- Be honest.

- Write lists.
- Go out for lunch with colleagues.
- Make sure everyone on the team has a role and feels part of the bigger picture.
- Be clear about your expectations of a team or what you can deliver.

It was a tricky balancing act to stay true to my most authentic self while also allowing myself to grow and attempt to embody the confidence, authority and panache one needs as the face of a brand such as *ELLE*. I vowed to be entirely honest with my colleagues throughout, and while I no doubt made some mistakes during my time in charge, I am proud that I remained committed to my core values as a gentlewoman: openness, empathy, kindness and fairness.

There was so much whispering and secrecy shrouding the application process and who was in line to be the new boss, it was an unsettling time for everyone I worked with. In our weekly meetings I encouraged people to share their anxieties and was open about my feelings too. It's crazy to think that at work we must have this 'professional' veneer that means we can't or won't say what we think, or behave as we would in other aspects of our lives.

Embracing vulnerability at work doesn't mean crying in the loos every day, that's just bad self-management and often the result of poor choices, lack of communication or not having taken proper care of yourself so that a situation spirals out of control, when you could have worked to solve it. Embracing vulnerability for a gentlewoman in this space means being empowered, no matter whether management or your co-workers encourage you to do so; to communicate honestly about how you feel, why you feel it, and offer possible solutions to a perceived problem.

I told the team when my big presentation for the job was, I told them I was nervous but excited, I said honestly I had no idea if I was a serious contender at all or if there was someone already in line for the job. I answered all their questions and addressed their concerns and said yes, of course I'd be crushed if I didn't get the job, but I'd be OK – I'd carry on happily as deputy editor again because like all of us on that team, I loved the magazine and everything it stood for.

A colleague I greatly respected asked to talk to me one day. She advised me to 'play my cards close to my chest'. She was probably right, I may have been seen as a greater threat, or a savvier operator, had I been more 'professional' (read 'guarded') about my experiences – I could have kept quiet about applying for the job at all. My cards were on the table for all to see, but that was me. It meant that whatever the outcome of this epic and on-going job application, I would never feel disappointed in myself. I couldn't have been any other way and been happy. I'd be able to hold my head high and feel satisfied that I hadn't allowed myself to be drawn into another dysfunctional relationship, this time with a job, that negated my sense of self.

When people are professionally insecure, then keeping secrets, or knowing something only a select few know, can be a compelling source of power. But it often leads to a parent/child style of leadership in that we must do what we are told and not ask why. A gentlewoman recognizes that all this does is breed an unhappy working environment where people are disempowered and waste time nervously wondering what is going on 'above' them rather than feeling safe and happy. I have always encouraged colleagues to connect with whomever they want to within a company or industry. If I start somewhere new, I do my research, find out who is doing interesting things in other departments, other companies and industry bodies, then I invite them to meet.

If you are a junior designer and you have a brilliant idea you'd like to tell the CEO, email her. People are so scared of the chain of command, of stepping outside the box their job title puts them in, but unless you are being manipulative or deliberately bypassing someone by contacting a senior member of staff off your own back, there is nothing to stop you.

If you don't cultivate an environment where everyone feels seen and heard and taking initiative is rewarded, people quickly lose interest and feel that as they are not able to exercise any real personal influence in contributing to the success of a company or project, they might as well not bother with anything above and beyond the bare minimum. This, in my opinion, leads to the greatest inefficiency and lack of creativity.

Two days after being made acting editor in chief, I received a summons from the big BIG boss in New York. Joanna Coles was an industry veteran, editor of *Marie Claire* UK and subsequently *Cosmopolitan* magazine in New York, and had starred in a reality TV show about US *Cosmopolitan* and then *Project Runway*, which made her famous internationally as a larger-than-life, no-nonsense, intimidating and demanding editor-in-chief. The email read, 'Meet me for dinner in Milan, tomorrow.' I would need all my gentlewoman resources for this one.

At a table by a big circular window overlooking the Duomo, in the ultra-chic Felix Lo Basso restaurant, I sat facing this editorial icon. Fashion thin and with a fierce crop of white-blonde hair, she was dressed in a black polo neck, cigarette pants and a sharp black blazer as she grilled me on everything from what I ate for breakfast to when I came out to my parents; the area I grew up in, the school I went to, how I intended to start a family, if I'd ever fired someone, my thoughts on style, celebrity, film – and then what I'd do with *ELLE*, my big ideas, how I'd make it famous, attract more readers, boost luxury advertising, and who I wanted on the cover, and who else, and who else, and who else...I recited my list of dream cover stars and she'd punctuate each of my suggestions with, 'Love her!', 'Eugh!', 'Cheap!', 'Yes, yes!', 'yes!', 'just had dinner with her!', 'Yes!', and to some of my suggestions, 'It worries me that you'd say that!' It was the conversational equivalent of an army boot camp – was I quick-thinking, business-minded, an authority on fashion, a confident leader and a sufficiently thick-skinned woman to handle the job? By the end of the meal, a risotto that I'd barely touched, I was exhausted and had a splitting headache. I'd been put through my paces like never before but I wasn't intimidated by her, I'd held my own and even made her laugh. I didn't bullshit or blag my way through but was confident in myself, and when she asked me if I was the right person for the job I really believed it when I answered, without hesitation, 'Yes.'

As the acting editor of *ELLE* I had to step it up. Yes, my advice to aspiring gentlewomen is not to have a work persona – an act you have to maintain – but to feel confident enough in yourself as a whole to be that person fully in all aspects of your life. But there are some jobs, like this one, for which it is necessary to dial up some of your natural characteristics and dial down others, while staying true to your core values. I had to dress the part, so I borrowed designer clothes from brands to wear to fashion shows and parties.

I sat front row, opposite Anna Wintour occasionally, who once actually took off her sunglasses to give me a look up and down, as if to say, 'And *who* are you?' I responded with a big smile and made sure to introduce myself to her and other glamazon international editors who must've been wondering who this new face on the frow was. 'You *do not* talk to Anna,' one stylist advised me, but why on earth not? I refused to cower to the conventions of 'fashion people'. I made conversation, and asked questions of my bench mates, fellow UK editors, some of whom, unlike me, were 'over' fashion month, exhausted by it all. They had been there, seen it, done it and were impossibly hard to impress. I on the other hand was wide-eyed and appreciative of every amazing show I got to see from the best seat in the house, for every 'gift' I was sent and glamorous dinner I was invited to. What amazing access, what fun and how privileged I felt to have been dropped into the white-hot centre of the scene.

I came across this passage in *The English Gentlewoman*, which sums up the attitude of some of the industry stalwarts I met. A gentlewoman, as my friend in 1861 agrees, should continue to relish opportunities, to enjoy life, and to show it:

> There is a class of being who are never satisfied; for them no company is good enough; nothing comes up to their expectations; everything is dull, everything is ill-managed. The last ball was delightful compared with this. All that we have not is excellent; the rooms are too large or too small; the lights are gas, they should have been wax; the refreshments are odious; there is not a partner in the room worth having. Let such remain away, nor sully the gaiety of the grateful heart by their jaundiced representations. Give me the free careless

creature whose soul is in her eyes; give me the flirt rather than these soured, fastidious beings who mingle the wormwood of their own natures with the pleasures of existence.

Staying true to myself in this world was not particularly popular with some. I rejected a way of being that, from what I observed, seemed to breed among those who lived and breathed it, insecurity, low self-esteem and a sense of paranoia at having said the wrong thing, behaved the wrong way, worn the wrong designer and so on.

I received feedback after one meeting with a luxury brand, held in their Bond Street showrooms, that I had come across as very 'confident'. The word was whispered as if even uttering it was offensive. Apparently there was some social code I wasn't aware of, and instead of talking normally to these people I should have approached it like a Japanese tea ceremony, not saying what I meant, dancing around the conversation delicately and not speaking freely. 'I wonder how many men they would accuse of being "confident",' was my response.

I was about two months into the job, and had been told I was through the first round of interviewing, when I realized some of the executives I was working with did not believe me to be the right person for the role. I wasn't 'fashion' enough, and never would be. There were clandestine meetings, overheard conversations, rumours, and a lot of secret WhatsApping, and while I knew all that was happening around me, I refused to let it detract from my enjoyment of the job. Because the fact was I was loving it. Never had I felt so able to put myself into my work – the magazines I edited at that time were labours of love, in which every story and shoot, every headline and quote, was something I personally believed in, and most of the team I was working with did too.

Some people didn't 'get' me, they didn't agree with my style of leadership or approach to editing the magazine; I knew who they were but I put them to the back of my mind.

As I was in the right place at the right time, it would fall to me to host the *ELLE* Style Awards. The event is a year in the planning, and we'd fly models, designers, film- and pop-stars in from all over the world to attend. Standing on stage that night, wearing a tuxedo that felt entirely right, I made a speech. I stood up in front of a room full of people – colleagues and celebrities, some of whom were rooting for me, some of whom weren't – and I said something about the passion and effort that went into creating *ELLE*. I said we all cared so much, and made the point that working for the magazine made us feel part of something important and that was a huge honour and privilege.

A gentlewoman's guide to making a speech

- Give yourself a full week to write your speech – take a day or two away from it then look at it again.
- Record yourself reading it aloud and listen to it every day when walking along to help memorize it.
- If you are thanking people in your speech show it to someone else who will know if you've remembered to thank everyone you need to.
- Never read from your iPhone.
- Don't try to be funny if it doesn't come naturally.

- Avoid holding sheets of paper when you deliver the speech – if you must have a printout hold it inside a hard-backed open file – your shaky hands will be less noticeable.
- Speak from the heart.

I chose to position myself on a table between Beth Ditto and Christine and the Queens, two queer heroes, and I had one of the best nights of my life, feeling that whatever happened with the job, I had achieved a huge career milestone; if I could host such a high-profile event and still feel that everything about that party from the decor to the music and the awards themselves reflected my sense of myself as a gentlewoman then I could do anything.

Unlike other celebrity awards ceremonies, which can be formal or pretentious, this one had an off-the-leash atmosphere, with acceptance speeches from stars such as Thandie Newton, Riz Ahmed, Beth Ditto, Vivienne Westwood and Debbie Harry becoming impassioned calls to action, addressing racism, immigration, environmentalism, queer power and the need for activism. No one expected such a politically charged event and it made for a spectacular energy. Tables were pushed aside, we kicked off our Louboutins and danced with a troupe of bearded drag queens into the early hours. I was still riding high after hosting what felt like the party of the year as I packed my suitcase ready to go to Paris Fashion Week.

I never made it.

'I'm afraid you haven't got the job,' one of the executives told me, 'and we think it best you don't go to Paris.' Like a scene from one of those fashiony chick-lit novels, I went home and unpacked my bag,

Cinders once more, arranging a courier to pick up all the designer clothes and return them to the ateliers. My time at the top was, as we say in fashion, OVAH. But what a great adventure it had been.

I stayed in the role for five months in total, eventually handing the reins over to *ELLE*'s long-standing fashion director and becoming her deputy editor. The next few months were a lesson in tact and humility. I graciously abdicated responsibility and told her that my job now was to support her. But it wasn't easy and I saw myself falling into the old patterns of behaviour of trying to please someone else. I was inauthentic – going along with decisions that I didn't necessarily agree with for an easy life.

Now I was maintaining an act, trying to say what I thought someone wanted to hear rather than what I believed. And it was exhausting. This was the most stressed I'd ever felt, even though in some ways the pressure was off, having to 'contain' myself wasn't part of my gentlewoman's manifesto.

Redundancy was inevitable, I suppose, but even though I was no longer loving my job in the way I had done, I still felt a personal attachment to the magazine and to the team of women who made it so brilliant. Leaving was hard and I realize now, looking back, that I went through the seven stages of grief (shock and denial, pain and guilt, anger and bargaining, depression, reconstruction, acceptance and hope), finally reaching acceptance about midway through my next role in a completely different industry.

As a gentlewoman you should care about your work, but care just enough, and not so much that your entire self is tied up with the thing you are doing or the company you are doing it for. I loved my job, maybe a bit too much, so when I left, it was like a break-up – only this time I was determined to make it a better one than the last break-up I'd been through. I sent cards to the people I'd worked closest with thanking them for their support, I sat in a café near the office one afternoon and emailed all my colleagues saying if anyone wanted to come and talk about what was happening with the redundancy, to join me there, and I organized my own leaving party, making a speech in which I said honestly how gutted I was to be going, how brutal redundancy had felt but how I knew it was the right thing for all of us and I was excited to move on. I also wished the new editor the very best, and she did me, and I knew we both meant it. There were no hard feelings.

How to leave a job like a gentlewoman

- Write thank-you cards to people you have enjoyed working with.
- Send an everyone email (the only time I ever advocate this) explaining that you are leaving in as honest a way as you are comfortable with (though keeping it professional, of course). If you don't do this someone else will send a perfunctory 'X is moving on to pastures new we wish her all the best' note, and you want to control your leaving narrative.
- Take the team you worked closest with out for lunch to explain why you are leaving in more detail.
- Plan a leaving party.
- Make a speech.
- Wear something fabulous on your last day.
- Keep in touch with people you care about, unfollow everyone else.

I promised myself to never again be inauthentic at work. When I accepted a role as a creative director at a global advertising agency, an industry I had no experience of but had been hired into as an experiment in 'doing things differently', this meant saying what I meant and meaning what I said. I challenged the lack of diversity in the creative department and asked more often than I'd have liked, 'Why are there only pictures of white men in this presentation? Why does this script have to star a man? Why are men in adverts people and women 'Women' – wives, mothers, girls playing football while on their period?' It's like Simone de Beauvoir writes in *The Second Sex*: 'Man is defined as a human being and a woman as a female – whenever she behaves as a human being she is said to imitate the male.'[6]

But it was my outsider's perspective that had got me the job in the first place and because I communicated my ideas and criticisms, I hope, as a gentlewoman – listening and understanding as well as challenging – I was able to be more effective than had I aggressively come across as the lesbian, feminist journalist with a chip on her shoulder and a copy of *The Second Sex* in her pocket.

I utilized soft power to forge meaningful relationships with my colleagues and speak to them individually. The behaviour change organization Changingminds.org explains soft power thus:

> *Soft power works not because it seeks to directly influence but through subtle and indirect means. At best, it is completely undetectable. It goes around obstacles. It seeks inattention. It inveigles its way in through neglected routes. It spreads without notice. Soft power does not ask. It shows. To create behaviour, just act in the way that you want others to act. Seeing your behaviour as worthy (and you as worthy), others may hence seek to imitate you.*[7]

It was imperative, then, for me to effect any real change in this company, or to really disrupt the status quo as I'd been hired to do, to forge good relationships with my colleagues. But it was one thing being myself in this whole new professional world and another finding 'my people'.

If you don't feel part of a gang, a collective or community all working together towards a shared goal, places of work can be lonely, particularly when hot-desking or when badly designed open-plan offices make it hard to get to know a group of people.

I was very far out of my comfort zone most of the time in advertising. I'd gone from working with a small team of women who had become some of my closest friends, to a vast network of mainly male creatives, strategists and account execs. I wasn't there to make friends, but when I did feel that spark of connection with someone, I realized it was beyond what we did as worker bees and more who we were outside the hive that formed the foundation of any meaningful relationship.

I knew it was on me to make the effort to introduce myself to people, set up lunch dates and coffees, tell my story and hear theirs, so in my first few weeks I invested time in seeking out others from across the business who I could relate to in this way. As soon as I had a little crew of people I could take on lunch dates and share ideas with, I felt far happier going to work each day.

So much of my identity had been connected to being a magazine editor, that when people asked 'what do you do?' I couldn't bring myself to say I worked in advertising without heavily caveating it. My job wasn't an extension of my personality any more.

I thought that because I had worked hard over the past few years to achieve a sense of self-worth that came from deep within me rather than from anything I appropriated externally, I would find the switch from a profession I cared passionately about to one I found interesting but was emotionally ambivalent about, to have little impact on my happiness. And in some ways I was right: I enjoyed my job – it was a great test in abandoning ego (I had no reputation to speak of in this industry) and being brave enough to admit what I didn't know and ask for help. Learning a new craft at that stage of my life was an exciting challenge but what I learned most profoundly during my year at the agency was that I *do* have to be able to invest something of myself into my job.

Maya Angelou said it better than I ever could: 'You can only become truly accomplished at something you love. Don't make money your goal. Instead pursue the things you love doing and then do them so well that people can't take their eyes off of you.'[8]

If a gentlewoman is to be truly happy at work, she has to care – not so much that it takes over – but to care just a bit more than enough, because her professional output is – as is her home, her style, her personal relationships and everything else – a reflection of herself.

Gentle suggestions for being at work

- Don't write anything in an email you wouldn't want read out in an all company meeting.
- Have friends but don't be cliquey – this isn't high school.
- Introduce yourself to the CEO next time you find yourself in a lift with them.
- Enjoy Mondays. It's dull and basic to say you hate going to work after the weekend. If you do, change something.
- If you realize you don't need to be in a meeting, politely excuse yourself.
- Ask if you really need a meeting or if you could just have a quick chat at someone's desk when possible.
- Avoid conference calls, particularly video conference calls, as much as possible.
- Ban jargon among you and your colleagues: CLOP, EOP, WFH.*
- WFH – sorry, 'work from home' – whenever you can.
- Don't wear headphones at your desk – you need to be engaged and part of the action.

* CLOP = 'close of play', EOP = 'end of play' and WFH = 'work from home'

CHAPTER 7

Being in clothes

Do you often feel the need to get rid of everything in your wardrobe and start again? Because having only new clothes – crisp white T-shirts, never-worn jeans, perfect underwear and unscuffed shoes – will somehow make you a box-fresh person too? Before bundling all your outfits into bin bags and dropping them at a second-hand store when you get that urge to purge, interrogate what you're really trying to get *rid* of. Have you had a difficult time at work or been through a break-up? Are you figuring out issues with your family? Are your friends dragging you down? Or do you feel unsatisfied with your body, unable to compete with the perfectly put-together Instagram influencers who always look so effortlessly on-trend (and impossibly good in a beret)? If that's the case it isn't the contents of your wardrobe that need to change.

You might be able to pull off a style refresh or a superficial makeover, but it is only once you are confident and complete and have wrestled the messiness of real life into something manageable, finding peace with all that you are and all that you will never be, that the clothes you wear will best reflect the woman you have become. However, if you are resolutely *not* mistaking the need to re-evaluate your life for a desire to re-evaluate your wardrobe, or if you have got to a place, finally, of feeling happy, stable and living well and now you need the clothes to match – then by all means rip everything out of your closet and with your gentlewoman hat on (*retrieves beret*) go through each item asking three simple questions:

1.   Do I ever wear this?
2.   Is it useful?
3.   Do I feel good in it?

If the answer to *at least* two of these questions is 'yes', then Shantay, it stays.* Everything else, sashays away – to a clothes bank, charity or to someone who will appreciate it.

I find it helpful to think about my clothes in terms of occasions and emotions because a sense of style should exist as an idea that is greater than the sum of its parts. A gentlewoman needs outfits that reflect when she is feeling 'cool' on evenings out, sharp, smart and powerful at work, relaxed and comfortable at the weekend, and she'll want to feel appropriately attired for a workout, a country walk, a beach holiday or a low-key trip to the supermarket.** Then, there are those fashion essentials, recommended in whatever variation suits you, that form the basis of a look. To insiders this is known as 'wardrobing', not to be confused with 'shrobing' (short for shoulder-robing, the act of draping a coat over your shoulders rather than putting your arms through the sleeves – do keep up!).

* 'Shantay you stay' is a phrase used on *RuPaul's Drag Race* when a contestant makes it through to the next round.
** I, personally, have a special tracksuit and baseball cap that renders me quite unrecognizable should I cross paths with an acquaintance while on a covert mission for crumpets.

Key pieces for a gentlewoman's wardrobe

- White shirt.

- Denim jeans.

- Blazer.

- Black dress or tuxedo.

- Winter coat.

- Polo neck.

- Good-quality plain black, white and grey T-shirts.

- Leather jacket.

- Chunky-knit jumper.

- White trainers.

- Classic black flat boots.

- A barely-there low heel.

- Silk slip dress to wear with leather jacket.

- Suede court shoes.

- Good seamless lingerie.

If a gentlewoman is careful and considered in every other aspect of her life, then her approach to style should be no exception. I *aspire* to a capsule wardrobe – a collection of a few essential items of clothing that don't go out of fashion, which can then be augmented with seasonal pieces. So ideally I would have one or two variations of the items listed above, plus good loungewear (cotton pyjamas, silk robe, soft cashmere sweaters), sportswear, power dressing and casual off-duty options, then seasonally specific ensembles that rotate into and out of my closet throughout the year. The reality is far from this, and my intentions to keep my drawers and rails as neat and seasonal as they are after one of my four wardrobe detox sessions a year are pathetically short lived, because I quickly accumulate more clothes than I have space for and because I choose to devote my spare time to pursuits that spark more joy than folding and hanging these clothes properly. Must. Try. Harder.

I may not have the patience to maintain the capsule wardrobe of my dreams, but what I do have is 'a look', which is more important. A gentlewoman should be confident in the way she presents herself to the world, and she should have a unique sense of style that feels instinctive and effortless. Here's how.

For a start, please don't ever regret any of your past fashion – let's not call them 'mistakes' – 'moments'. Celebrate them and allow them to remain a part of the patchwork (and wow, did I love a bit of patchwork) that has made you who you are today. Experimenting with different looks as we mature is a visual representation of the ways in which we remain knee-deep in the quagmire of 'finding ourselves' for a long time, before wading out finally (in better shoes), with a look that sticks and a self we like.

But developing a look of your own means disregarding what the other people at work or in the gym, at the school gates or on campus are wearing and building your style around your sense of self, not the other way round. Be inspired by others, sure, but to really survive and thrive in the world today dress authentically and for no one but yourself.

It's hard not to judge people by the clothes they wear; they can be a shop window to our soul and also signifiers of social status and so much more. We no longer live in a world where assumptions about identity based on one's fashion sense can be as readily made as they once were. This means we can have more fun with clothes and not feel limited by the uniform our 'tribe' dictates. 'Fit in' because you have something deeper in common with a group of people than a brand of leggings.

Wear what makes you feel good, what makes you feel *you*, and if that means making a few faux pas along the way, experimenting and doing your best to break free from that temptation to be a style chameleon, then so be it.

Everything we choose to wear is a performance of ourselves, so don't feel that it's ever too late to change your style if it no longer reflects the woman you are. If you have split up with a partner or quit a job that was making you unhappy, and have done the work necessary to move onwards and upwards, becoming a gentlewoman, then invest in a new look that better suits this new you.

Meet a gentlewoman

Elizabeth Day is an author and journalist and the woman behind the popular *How to Fail* book and podcast[1].

How did you dress when you were in an unhappy relationship?
Well, in my specific case I was married to a man 11 years older than me. So, I felt like I needed to dress 'older' than I was because I felt inferior to him. These are not justifiable or rational feelings, but that was how I felt. I dressed in an uptight way, as if the corsetry of my clothes was actually keeping my emotions tempered down. In terms of style, they were quite submissive and quiet, and I think that was

representative of the fact that I'd got myself into a situation where I didn't feel like I had a voice in that relationship. Also, because I didn't feel like my voice was being listened to professionally. I was in a job that I was equally increasingly unhappy in.

So, who would you say you were dressing for at that time?
For my ex-husband at points, and I was dressing up and seeking to disguise my own insecurity. I was dressing for a world in which I wanted to be taken more seriously than I felt like I was being taken. So I was probably dressing for people that I thought were judging me, and generally they were older people. Generally older men, because that happened to be the industry I was in at that given time.

What did you feel when you saw yourself?
When I looked in the mirror at the time, which was also a time when I was seeking to diminish myself physically – a symptom of stress and hyper control – I was always quite critical of my weight and size. Now when I look back on photos of myself at that time in my life I think I look really sad. I think if you look sad then you end up looking a bit older than you are. I was trying to contain all of these things, and all of that mad stress presented itself in degrees of control. I don't look back and see a happy and relaxed person, which I think is key to liking yourself.

When did you realize that your sense of style wasn't reflecting your sense of self?
My marriage ended in 2015 and I went to LA for three months. Because I wasn't working in an office any more it just felt like I could wear exactly what I wanted. By the end of those three months I realized that I had relaxed and liked what I was wearing; I felt

very good about myself there. Being liberated from an unhappy relationship, combined with a different style aesthetic in LA – cotton, flip-flops etc. – all of that made me realize how I liked to dress. So, when I came back to the UK I still tried to have that element of easy dressing. I started wearing a lot more trainers and sweatshirts, and jeans that were looser but cut off at the ankle, rather than very tight very skinny-fitting clothes.

Was it quite destabilizing to think, OK, if this sense of style isn't me, then what is?
I definitely remember a time when I felt like I was losing myself in my ex-marriage. I needed help. I remember going to a friend and being, like, 'Tell me what to wear.' He took me shopping a couple of times because I just genuinely didn't know what I wanted in my life emotionally, and that was reflected in the not knowing what I needed in clothes.

So once you had done the work on yourself, did finding a way to dress that better suited you come more naturally?
I actually just got rid of a lot of clothes that made me sad when looking at them. I remember the top I was wearing when I had a miscarriage. I was like, 'I can't have that any more.' I got rid of a lot of clothes, and that was helpful. When I was buying more clothes, I was like, 'Oh well, I don't have to dress like that person because actually the person who I thought I was would have stayed married, but I hadn't done that so I had to ask myself, 'Who am I and who do I want to be?' So I started buying clothes that were more in tune with my LA self, a progression that included starting to wear colour.

For most of my twenties I was 'preppy' in button-down shirts, sweaters and chinos and *then*, just in time for my career in fashion magazines to take off, I slipped on a duck-egg blue Joseph suit, with a plain white T-shirt and white Stan Smiths and looked in the mirror and felt, finally, this was me.

Suits in different colours, worn mainly with trainers, sometimes with loafers or brogues and very occasionally with a heel, has become my signature look and finding it coincided with me finding the happiest, most complete and comfortable way of being myself in all aspects of life. Such suits have become my work uniform and the look has also helped me develop a more relaxed style that best suits weekend or after hours 'me' too. The look is smart but not formal, and androgynous in a way I can dial up or down depending on how I feel like performing my gender identity that day. But most importantly when I wear a freshly pressed suit I *feel* good. The way I understand myself emotionally aligns with the way I present myself outwardly, and this is what we should strive for in our fashion choices more than anything else.

Women who lack such self-knowledge or are struggling to like themselves can struggle equally to feel that they have a coherent and consistent sense of their style. If you are just starting out in your journey to becoming a gentlewoman, you may find that an outfit wears you more than you wear it. Perhaps it is also tempting to buy expensive designer items in the hope that they will add value to you as a person or stand for something you want (wealth, success, fashionableness). But owning designer clothes and accessories does not make you stylish. Instead, it is all about the time and effort a gentlewoman puts into genuinely finding a look that suits her personality.

Buy something 'designer' because it is well made, because you love it and will keep it for ever, not because of its logo. Anyone with enough money can buy a Prada handbag, but a gentlewoman is not 'anyone', she is confidently, joyfully and uniquely herself. If she does shop designer she mixes such items with high-street, vintage or clothes by less well-known independent labels to make the look her own. She does not go in for garish displays of brand names, preferring the quiet quality of beautiful clothes and accessories created by a designer she knows about and respects.

It is by the same token that I'd encourage you not to wear a slogan T-shirt or one featuring a band, a quote or a person you know nothing about. I once asked a colleague at *ELLE* wearing a Bella Freud 'Ginsberg is God' jumper who Ginsberg was and she didn't know. But the next time she wore it she had memorized the opening passage of Allen Ginsberg's epic poem 'Howl' and recited 'I saw the best minds of my generation…' to me, which made her eminently more cool than the £290 jumper did in my eyes.

Working for luxury lifestyle and fashion magazines helped me understand fashion as a rich cultural narrative. I had always been interested in it, but sitting alongside passionate stylists and picture editors every day opened my eyes to the way the right woman in the right place in the right combination of clothes can create an iconic, powerful image and tell a story as all great art can. It is worth really looking at shoots in good magazines, not just flicking through the pages, because the effort and craftsmanship that goes into them creates something quite beautiful.

In *The Picture of Dorian Gray*, Oscar Wilde writes:

Beauty is a form of Genius – is higher, indeed, than Genius, as it needs no explanation. It is one of the great facts of the world, like sunlight, or springtime, or the reflection in the dark waters of that silver shell we call the moon. It cannot be questioned. It has divine right of sovereignty.[2]

Those who define themselves as intellectuals and proudly uninterested in fashion, make-up and the like believe wrongly that 'beauty' is frippery. They think it superficial and meaningless. But a gentlewoman is astute enough to understand profoundly that being interested in clothes, trends, or celebrity does not negate an interest in more 'worthy' intellectual pursuits. In fact, a healthy passion for both high and low culture and the ability to apply the same powers of critical reasoning to a reality TV show as a piece of philosophy is what marks a gentlewoman out from a crowd.

'Fashion' is political. Style on the other hand is personal and the warp and weft of these together produces something any smart woman should covet. So learn about fashion, don't just read naff 'who wore it better' celebrity critiques, but seek out the weighty writers contextualizing our social moment with their fashion stories. They will help you understand trends, where they come from, what they mean and how – if you wish – you can partake in them.

A gentlewoman's fashion reading list

Robin Givhan – Fashion Editor, the *Washington Post* (@RobinGivhan).

Jess Cartner-Morley – Associate Editor (fashion) the *Guardian* (@JessC_M).

Cathy Horyn – Critic at Large for *New York Magazine*'s 'The Cut' (@CathyHoryn).

Jo Ellison – Fashion Editor, the *Financial Times (@jellison).*

However respectful I was of the fashion world and my colleagues who inhabited it, I was never considered 'one of them' because my path to the top job had been via writing (or 'wordy things' as one fashion director I worked with jokingly – I think – called them) not images. The pursuit of beauty, when you factor in stress, insecurity, anxiety, gossip, the pressure of deadlines and the importance placed on one's position on a wooden bench at a fashion show, can turn ugly.

When I was editing *ELLE* I was lent clothes by designer brands. I was invited into stores and able to pick whatever I wanted to wear. It was an inconceivable privilege and I found that with the amazing clothes I borrowed, I was also lent an armour that steeled me for the 'scene' I was entering as quite the outsider. I wonder what the long-term effect of borrowing all my clothes could have had on my identity. Would I have 'shrobed' my way into a diva-ish ego, slipped hubris on like a pair of Louboutins and let self-aggrandizement be a thing I carried in my Celine bag? I wasn't in it long enough to find out.

Dressing for work is important, whatever your industry, and even when I'm working freelance or from home I will undertake the ritual of 'getting ready'. I don't WFH (sorry!) in one of my best suits, that would be a waste, but I shower, do my hair, moisturize (though I take the opportunity to give my skin a make-up-free day) and wear something that makes me feel as though I'm ready to work, not to snuggle up on the sofa.

Ideally, if not in a job that has a uniform, a gentlewoman puts some of herself and personality into her work wear. Thinking because you have a serious job you must wear serious (grey, dull, generic) clothes is seriously silly. Looking 'smart' doesn't mean looking boring. Likewise, if your natural predilection is for a style that is laid back to the point of scruffy, think more about the image you want to exude at work. Remember – be seen, be a contender, don't count yourself out by dressing like you don't care. I do believe there is wisdom in the old saying, 'Dress for the job you want, not the job you have.'

One of my personal fashion icons is Iris Apfel, who at the time of writing is 97 years old. She is lauded for her eccentric fashion sense: giant owl-like reading glasses and oversized costume jewellery. She famously said: 'Great personal style is an extreme curiosity about yourself.'[3]

Perhaps you haven't got to this place of allowing curiosity about (and I'd also add 'kindness' towards) yourself to shape your sense of style and are still figuring out what suits you or what you *think* you should wear because it's in magazines, on Instagram or what the other women you identify with seem to like to wear. Finding your look is a process – it takes time.

Style tips from a gentlewoman

Nicky Yates is a fashion director for magazines and a personal stylist for Hollywood actresses. Here she shares her style top tips:

1. Collect images of people whose style you like: models, celebrities, friends, influencers, even people you don't know on Instagram. Tear things out of magazines or take screen grabs. Use this for inspiration not emulation.

2. I have a policy of one in one out, so any time I get anything new, something has to go. I always have to have the same number of hangers in my wardrobe. Otherwise it just becomes overwhelming.

3. Never buy a new item of clothing without being sure you have something that goes with it. Think about what you might have at home that'll work with the thing you want to buy or buy something new on the same shopping trip.

4. Alterations are key; people don't do it as often as they should. Most boutiques (not high street, though, sadly) offer alteration services now. If you think, 'God, I love that', but it's the wrong length – don't be afraid to buy things and get them tailored to make them your dream item.

5. Put your money towards good shoes and bags and then you can basically do the high street for the rest of it.

6. Only ever have one thing doing the talking. If you want to wear a bold dress, then everything else should be low key – keep the hair and make-up quite fresh.

7. Be bold and experiment with your style when you're on holiday and you're away from your normal routine. Buy

something that you wouldn't usually buy, wear it and think about how you feel in it. You need to give yourself a chance to try something out without everyone in the office looking at you and asking if you've got a hot date or a job interview. It can be a shock seeing yourself in a new look. So, I'd always say give it a go on holiday.

8. If a trend fits around what you normally would wear that's great – but the most stylish people I know don't follow trends, they have their own style regardless.

Busyness often leads you to 'throw' an outfit together in a rush and not really put as much thought into clothes as a gentlewoman should. You will end up wearing something crumpled, pulled in a panic from the bottom of your 'floordrobe' and teamed with the first pair of clean jeans you can find and then finished with inappropriate footwear because just before leaving the house you decide you don't look smart enough so swap your flats for heels you can barely walk in.

When you enter a room, be it a bar or an office, after getting dressed in such a frantic way you will not exude calm or confidence. So respect yourself enough to put as much care into your outfits as you do everything else.

Try laying out the clothes you plan to wear the next day the night before. Take a moment to check your diary – what's happening at work, what's happening socially, will you need a change of shoes to run to a parents' evening or a different pair of earrings to make you feel fancier for a first date? Check the weather and check that the outfit you think you want to wear is actually clean, ironed and ready. Think about the whole week – do you definitely want to wear this tomorrow and not on Wednesday when you have that important meeting? The ritual of laying out clothes in advance sets your intention for the next day or the evening out ahead. What do you want to get out of this experience, what mood will you bring to it?

Perhaps I have more in common with the author of *The English Gentlewoman* than I'd thought, as in 1861 she too proposes:

> *Her wardrobe should be so arranged that everything of last night's attire is put in its place, and each article intended for the morning's use at hand [...] It is the mark of a true gentlewoman to be dressed with a competent degree of dispatch so as to come forth from her chamber neat and finished in her attire.*[4]

In an effort to avoid style complacency, and to stay engaged with the positive act of choosing what to wear, I suggest you don't repeat an outfit in a week. This might feel 'extra' to you, but not making the effort shows a lack of either planning or imagination. Of course, you'll need *enough* options not to wear the same outfit twice in seven days, and that means shopping.

It is healthy to question your motives for shopping. When it's me at my laptop with a large glass of Malbec after a tiring day, feeling that 'oh why not?' tingle under the skin, making me 'add to basket' with gay abandon, I'm wary of the real reason behind my desire to buy buy buy! More often than not it's to fill a void that could be satiated by talking to a friend, having a bath, reading a book or eating a nice meal – all of which are cheaper, and better for the environment.

'Retail therapy' is a cliché of womanhood, which along with our apparent obsession with Prosecco has kept many a novelty mug designer in business. But there is much truth in it (retail therapy, not Prosecco, which any sensible person will have swapped for Crémant a long time ago). That sense that something is missing, the 'lack' that I have personally felt as a result of grief, guilt and an unfulfilling relationship, is temporarily allayed by purchasing the accoutrements of a good life. Just like alcohol, drugs, sex, cigarettes, food or exercise, shopping can plaster over the gaps in oneself.

Abraham Maslow was an American psychologist who in 1943 came up with a 'hierarchy of needs',[5] which has resonated with people ever since. Beyond what we must have for basic survival and physical safety, he categorizes a human's remaining needs as love and belonging, including the necessity of being accepted and understood, and then self-esteem, that is the need to feel of value and to count for something. The fifth and final 'level' in his hierarchy is self-fulfilment, basically what we are aiming for in becoming 'gentlewomen'. He cites 'completeness, joyfulness, unity and understanding' as among the characteristics of such 'self-actualized' people. It's unlikely that Maslow had buying a pair of Balenciaga boots in mind when he considered how we may respond when we are deprived of such needs, but desiring something and then acquiring it is hugely satisfying and can certainly provide that sense of 'completeness and joyfulness' when nothing else in life we desire appears as easy to obtain. According to experiments by researchers at the University of Michigan and their resulting report in the *Journal of Consumer Psychology*:

> *People often shop when feeling sad[...] Sadness is strongly associated with a sense that situational forces control the*

outcomes in one's life, and thus we theorized that the choices
inherent in shopping may restore personal control over one's
environment and reduce residual sadness. Sadness, more than
any other emotion, is associated with a perceived deficiency
in personal control over one's environment. People who are
sad are especially likely to view outcomes as governed by
situational forces and chance, rather than their own actions.
To the extent that these appraisals create or maintain the
experience of sadness, aspects of shopping that restore a sense
of personal control over one's environment may subsequently
reduce residual sadness.[6]

It is so easy to shop without thinking; to have one eye on the
TV and another on your phone as you scroll through the 'just in'
items at your favourite online retailer. We don't even need to type
in our credit card details any more, a step which added a layer of
admin and time to really think about the purchase we were making.
Now a mere tap of the finger or face recognition can be all that's
needed to drop our hard-earned cash.

A gentlewoman is an advocate of mindful shopping. This means
shopping as an activity that you are fully present in, and while
online shopping is certainly more time efficient, actually going
into shops, feeling the weight – literal and metaphorical – of what
you want to buy is one way to be gently engaged in the process. If
you find yourself browsing online while distracted, make an effort
to step away from the screen and do something else – fix a drink,
rearrange the cushions on your sofa, use the phone to call someone
for a chat. Come back to it once you have thought about what you
are looking to buy and why. Writing a list of items and reasons you
want/need them in a notebook can help rationalize your choices.

When it comes to a higher price item I find putting it in my online basket and then waiting 24 hours before assessing if I still want it helps me avoid buying something I'll regret or could have done without. It could also be a good idea to remove the stored payment details on your phone and personal computer that make it dangerously quick and easy to click 'buy now'. And if you're really serious about mindful shopping deactivate Apple Pay, as even the act of getting your purse from your bag and taking out a bank card can make you think twice about a purchase you could have barely consciously tapped to make.

Mindful shopping also means considering the environmental impact and ethical provenance of your purchasing choices.

How to shop more mindfully

Sarah Ditty is Policy Director for Fashion Revolution, a global movement across more than 100 countries campaigning for a cleaner, safer and fairer fashion industry. Here she outlines 5 key practices that might help you to embrace a more mindful approach to clothes shopping.

1. **Buy less**

   Over 150 billion garments are produced each year, which is equivalent to nearly 20 brand-new items of clothing for every person on the planet. Meanwhile, studies show that people don't wear over half of the clothing they own, and Britons send 235 million items of clothing to landfill each year.

2. **Wear your clothes longer**

   If you wear an item of clothing for just nine months longer, it would reduce carbon, water and waste footprints by around 20–30 per cent each – but only if new purchases are avoided.

3. **Care for your clothes better**

   Stains, tears and missing buttons do happen but clothes worth wearing are worth repairing. Learn how to sew on a new button or patch a hole in your favourite item. Not only does it save you money and make your garment last longer, but you will feel empowered by your new-found ability to fix something yourself.

4. **Support small, independent and values-driven designers, brands and artisan communities**

   Where you put your hard-earned money matters. An increasing number of young fashion designers and brands are making clothes in a more sustainable way. Seek them out and buy their wares, if you can afford to do so.

5. **Ask questions**

   Fashion Revolution's mantra is: 'Be curious. Find out. Do something.' Being a responsible consumer starts with one simple question we should be asking every brand we buy: Who made my clothes?

In one of my favourite Samuel Beckett plays, *Happy Days*, a woman sits on stage buried up to her neck in sand. She is existing, barely, in a hinterland where all reality is crumbling as even language starts to lose its meaning. The question at the heart of the piece is: when you have no one to see yourself in relation to, how can you validate your existence? How can you stay alive when there is literally nothing or no one to live for? It sounds bleak but it's actually very funny and one of the passages from the play that has most stayed with me is when, in spite of her absurd circumstances, Winnie insists: 'Keep yourself nice, Winnie, that's what I always say, come what may, keep yourself nice.'

> *What now? Words fail. There are times when even they fail.*
> *Is that not so [...] that even words fail at times?*
> *What is one to do then until they come again? Brush and comb*
> *the hair if it has not been done, or [...] trim the nails if they*
> *are in need of trimming.*[7]

At its deepest level this is why taking care of oneself matters. As long as we mind about the image we project, and there is a reason to brush our hair, cut our nails or do any number of personal grooming rituals that help us feel 'presentable', it means we are active in the way we choose to *be* in the world, or in a Beckettian sense, *exist*.

When my cousin Billie was in a hospice, in the final month of her life, she was still visited weekly by a beauty therapist who massaged her hands and painted her nails. The therapist treated most of the female patients and at the time I thought this was futile and just desperately sad, but I was wrong. And I want you to understand why, because what it really demonstrated was a desire not to let oneself go until the last breath. This is truly soft power in the hardest times. To live your fullest, take the best care of yourself and understand profoundly that the need to 'come what may, keep yourself nice' is an attitude to life, and far more about self-preservation than self-indulgence.

I'm not advocating an obsession with body maintenance, more a consciousness about *what* you choose to do to help you feel most yourself in your body and *why*. You might be someone who chooses never to shave your armpits, or you might be someone who schedules a monthly itinerary of waxing, plucking, facials, blow-drys and Shellac. Neither approach is 'better' or more gentlewomanly than the other, as long as the result makes you feel you can inhabit your body most authentically and you have put thought into 'taking care of yourself', even when that means consciously deciding *not* to do something such as shave or wear a bra.

We *live* in clothes; so having a strong sense of personal style as a gentlewoman is about more than the contents of your wardrobe, it is the content of your character.

Gentle suggestions for being in clothes

- Give your make-up bag a makeover every six months.
- Stand up straight.
- Always look in a full-length mirror before leaving the house.
- Don't wear shoes you can't walk in.
- Follow dress codes but add your own flair.
- Wear a watch.
- Be generous with compliments, but mean them.
- If someone says something nice about your outfit, say 'thank you' rather than being self-deprecating.
- Never wear flesh-coloured tights.
- Iron shirts.

CHAPTER 8

Being a family

As a caring, emotionally switched-on and empathetic person, it's easy to feel that your personal happiness is contingent on everyone else you love being happy too. But, like Sisyphus, the disgraced king in ancient Greek mythology whose punishment is to push a boulder up a hill so that it rolls down and he must start again, for ETERNITY, making other people's happiness your 'purpose' is futile and exhausting. Taking responsibility for your family's holistic well-being might be a kind of Barry's Boot Camp for the soul, but while Sisyphus certainly achieved his step count and calorie burn each day, he was miserable as hell.

'I'm OK if you're OK' is not a good mantra to live by because other people are Rubik's Cubes of complicated desires and instincts. Each one of them views the world, and their starring role in it, in an impenetrably unique way. However many variations I try, I will never make the coloured squares fit together in the same way *they* do. And the more people you are lucky enough to love and care about, the more impossible variations there are.

When it comes to the inevitable emotional ups and downs of life (I'm not talking serious dramas here, more low-level interruptions to people's general equilibrium), 'I'm OK, whether you are or not' is a far healthier approach to family life. Because a gentlewoman should understand that the only person she can truly change or control is herself. Gentlewomen work to become stable, content, self-actualized people not so we can smugly slap #blessed on our lives but so that we have a good base enabling us to be the most supportive and uplifting we can be for others, without taking their issues and anxieties on as our own.

The ancient Chinese philosopher and teacher Confucius explained it thus:

> *To put the world in order, we must first put the nation in order; to put the nation in order, we must first put the family in order; to put the family in order; we must first cultivate our personal life; we must first set our hearts right.*

From the moment I saw the 'grown-ups' in my family as vulnerable, probably when I received that phone call from my mum saying, 'Your dad's gone', I decided it was my job to fix everybody but myself. I wanted to rescue my family from grief and stop anything bad from ever happening again. I never asked for help from them because that would have meant burdening them with my unhappiness too. Instead, I tried to drag them with me to a place I thought we could get to if we just persevered, where everything would be OK and we'd all be 'happy'. But I didn't even know what that meant. Out of all the things I have tried to challenge about my own way of being in and understanding the world as I've endeavoured to become more of a gentlewoman, most transformative has been overcoming the idea that I would not be able to 'find my joy' until everyone else in my close family found theirs. I recognize now that I needed to put my energy into processing and recovering from loss in my own way, and figuring out what 'happiness' was for me. I needed to give my family the space to do the same and not expect them to work to my timescale.

Integral to becoming a gentlewoman has been questioning all of my actions. Of course, we wish good things to happen to everyone we care about and it is impossible not to be affected when the opposite is true, but I realized that although it came with good intentions, wanting other people to be happy so that I could be was selfish not selfless.

Asserting soft power with your family means showing rather than telling. So, I got *myself* to a better place and began acting consistently with what I believed. I stopped trying to control the nuances of their individual understanding of a situation, forcing them to 'look on the bright side' and find happiness when there were other, perhaps more important things they needed to find in their own way first. My job was to offer support and understanding. I could be kind and do practical things to help make their lives easier, but I couldn't make them better.

It's taken me a long time to accept that life *is* suffering, but living well, liking myself, falling in love, being happy and successful are things that can happen *in spite* of this. I have left the boulder at the bottom of the mountain and walked away because I was only punishing myself.

Being a gentlewoman doesn't exempt you from hard times, it should make you better able to get through them, but part of your success in this is knowing when you need to ask someone else for help: for them to listen, offer advice or turn up at your door with a bottle of good gin, tonic and limes. I now treat those I am closest to how I expect to be treated and assume, unless clear otherwise, that they are robust enough to support me when I need it, without feeling that asking for help means I'm adding to their woes.

It is indeed true that 'you can't choose your family', but a gentlewoman chooses how much to give to them.

Perhaps you don't feel you can be the woman you have become in every other aspect of your life around the family you grew up with, because either they still treat you as the person they knew or you fall into old patterns of behaving like that around them. Worse still, you can't talk honestly about your life, perhaps because of your gender or sexual identity, the work you do or lifestyle you enjoy because you will be aggressively ostracized or quietly misunderstood. If your family dynamic falls somewhere on this spectrum then I'm afraid there is no single 'solution', because unlike other relationships, with friends, partners or even a job, which are tricky but achievable to let go of if not serving your best interests, we often can't help but love the people who raised us even when they don't deserve it.

Family can be so complicated, so riddled with love and hate, guilt and resentment, a child's desire to please their parents and a parent's desire to vicariously achieve what they never could through their children, there is not a clear path out of the woods. I would hope that throughout this process of learning and then becoming who you are, being confident, consistent and aspiring to live a joined-up life rich with kindness and compassion, that you will be better equipped to deal with it.

How to survive family rejection

Paris Lees is a writer, broadcaster and British *Vogue* columnist

What was it like trying to explain to your family that you are a trans woman?

I was clear from a verbal age: I'm a girl. I kept that up for quite a few years. When I was about nine or ten, after years of not being believed, having it hammered into me by my parents that 'no you cannot be this, this is not OK', I believed them. I was like, 'OK, well they are right and I am wrong.' I just tried as best as I could to blend in and go inside myself. I think that is the saddest thing really; I was at the age when most people are just beginning to discover themselves, meanwhile a lot of LGBT people are learning how to hide themselves. Everything was shrouded in shame. It wasn't until I got to the age of 14 that I got that rebellious rush and I thought, 'F*** this, I can do what I want!' I have friends who came from middle-class backgrounds who have been very privileged in many ways, but they felt like they had all of this love from their families, and it was almost a burden. It kept them in the closet for a lot longer, because they felt like they had a good relationship to lose. My relationship with my parents wasn't good, but it freed me to be who I was sooner because I'd got nothing to lose. I transitioned when I was very young because I wasn't beholden to anybody. I didn't fear family rejection because there wasn't the 'Chocolate Box' family to lose.

Should people who are lucky enough to come from a supportive family be more conscious of the fact that not everyone has?

This is something I struggle with every single day. How do we get people to empathize with something that they haven't been through? It is like trying to explain grief to someone who has never lost someone close to them. They can get it theoretically but that's it. The thing I envy the most about people who have got good relationships with their families is that they know no matter what happens – if their house burns down or Storm Troopers come and kick in the doors – they can get in a car or jump on a train, or walk if they have to, to a certain street and a certain house and knock on the door at any hour of the day and they will be welcomed in, and there will be love for them and a bed for them and there will be food. I don't know how you can communicate what it's like not to have that to people who do. But I'd urge you to please be mindful that some of us spend our lives walking on a tightrope knowing that there is no safety net. This is why trans kids who are not supported by their families are much more likely to end up homeless, depressed and having issues with addiction. A stable family is the single biggest influence in a person's life and can signify whether or not they are going to be happy, healthy and successful.

What advice do you have for people who have grown up with a family that has never unconditionally accepted them for who they are?

Sometimes people are crap – and they let down those they should be there for the most. Don't internalize it. If they are rejecting you, they are wrong. Either they will one day come to see this or they won't. But you are valid. You are fine. It is incredibly painful to be rejected by family. But hopefully one day you will reach a stage when you can believe you were right and you did the right thing. I have had a lot of friends who would pander to their parents, because they loved them – they would let them get away with stuff. One of many reasons I didn't speak to my dad for ten years was because he wouldn't call me by female pronouns. Some people would have said, 'Oh well, he's still my dad' and got on with it. There is an argument for working with your family while they work through the issues. For me, I just felt like respecting myself and asserting my identity was much more important. I thought, 'I am not going to be in a room with somebody who isn't going to take me seriously.' And now he does. Sometimes you have to really stand strong in who you are and what you deserve and what you are prepared to take from other people. The thing that really used to annoy me – when I was really affected by my dad – was when people would say, 'Oh but he is your dad, you know, he does love you.' I'm sorry, this doesn't make it better; this makes it worse.

Finding out, shortly after I had graduated from university, that my dad had a secret life with other women was a shock, to say the least. Suddenly my memories of a happy childhood and everything I thought I knew about my parents was turned upside down. What was real?

Families have secrets. When my grandad died, my mum and her two sisters found a locked trunk in his attic that had a note stuck to it reading, 'In the event of my death burn this box.' What would you have done? Incinerated it so that whatever secrets it concealed went up in smoke and the memory of him wouldn't be tarnished, or defy his orders from beyond the grave and open the box in an effort to get to know the truth about the real man? They burned it, as requested. I felt that I'd opened a trunk full of secrets once my mum told me honestly about the demise of her marriage to my dad, but as Romy sings in 'Brave for You':

> *There are things I wish I didn't know*
> *I try my best to let them go*[1]

Often it is a desire to protect those we love that sees us resorting to telling white lies or keeping secrets. But is this really the way to protect each other? I'd vote for putting 'gentle candour' at the heart of our families and challenging ourselves to be honest about situations it might have been tempting to lock in that trunk. Telling the truth doesn't have to be brutal if delivered at the right time and with the kindness and empathy of a gentlewoman. It is healthier for everyone to know what really happened, and how we really felt about it.

As we become the elders in our families, I think it is our duty to do away with the cult of the unsaid. Let's try to be the most honest we can be with relatives and initiate the kind of conversations that bring festering issues out from under the carpet.

Dealing with your parents separating as an adult is no easier than when it happens at an earlier age. It's different, of course; you're not shuttling between homes in the same way children with separated parents do, or having sad dinners in Pizza Express with them where you're told that Mummy and Daddy still love you very much. But you must still come to terms with the fact that the people you may love most in the world no longer love each other.

My instinct at the time was to go full *Parent Trap* and try to fix their relationship. I remember talking to my mum, suggesting she say this or that to him, that they keep talking, that if my dad would just meet up with her one more time he'd realize he'd made a mistake. But there was nothing I could do. After 23 years of it being all about me, it wasn't about me at all any more. They'd raised me well together, and now I was cooked they had to figure out what they wanted from the rest of their lives.

We all get to this point of realizing our parents are fallible people and it is up to us to re-establish our relationship with them on a more even ground.

A gentlewoman's guide to getting to know your parents as people

- Ask them about their previous partners.
- Meet their friends.
- Find out what scares them.
- Get a little bit drunk with them.
- Dance together.
- Go on a mini-break (book separate rooms).
- Look at never-before-seen photos of them when they were younger.
- Watch their favourite film and read their favourite book.

There comes a time for most of us when we become the parent to our parents: making all the arrangements, paying for everything and checking up on their health. I'm surprised by how many women my age say that they still revert to 'being a kid' when they are with their family. I imagine it's nice to be waited on, indulged, and to be able to be sulky or slam some doors for old times' sake, but in the spirit of living a 'joined-up life', proudly be your best self with your family and treat them with the same charm and respect you would others, however mad they drive you.

It can be hard to accept a parent–child role reversal is happening, particularly if you've been cosseted by your parents or carers for longer than you should have been. But, assuming they have spent a number of years looking after you, it is only fair that you eventually return the favour. When it comes to it, try not to resent the change in dynamic, because it is not easy for parents to relinquish their control either. Understanding what a challenge to their sense of self-worth ageing and letting go of their children can bring, and how this may manifest in their behaviour, will help you navigate your changing relationship in the best way for all of you. So will keeping in touch as much as necessary (but not so much it becomes kindling to anxiety and stress). Be grateful if you have brothers or sisters to share in this process with you, just stay conscious of the balance of responsibility and initiate the conversations and plans that will make sure no one feels that it is all 'on them'.

Attempting to find validation, or the answer to questions *about* myself *within* myself, helped me get over the rudderlessness I had started to feel after my parents split up and moved out of the flat I'd grown up in, and then when Billie died a few years later and I lost that mirror to our childhood. One of the things I have missed most about my older cousin is jointly constructing the stories of our childhood. Without her I can feel the sharp Polaroid edges of times I thought I'd never forget softening, blurring, threatening to disappear.

I have so much respect for people who keep a narrative diary because this is the best way to hold on to the precious stories that have made you who you are. If you don't have the patience for this, it's easier to spend time putting photos, digital or print, into an order that's easily accessible so that you always have this record of your personal history whether you have siblings to share it with or not. You could even write little captions for each image so that when you return to them in decades to come, or when in your absence generations beneath you stumble across them, a sense of the story behind the moment prevails.

The 13th-century Persian poet Rumi wrote: 'Don't be satisfied with stories, how things have gone with others. Unfold your own myth.' We all have our own versions of the past. We understand the things that happen to us as a family through our individual 'lenses' and that can make it hard to get to what is actually true and what is one person's interpretation of the truth. It is easier to be with family if you accept that we are all unfolding our own myth. Challenging someone's version of events is likely to cause conflict – maybe you experienced the same thing differently, but appreciating that their experience is equally valid can be a useful strategy in maintaining the equilibrium a gentlewoman seeks in family matters. In the 1800s the Danish philosopher Søren Kierkegaard, wrote: 'It is perfectly true, as the philosophers say, that life must be understood backwards. But they forget the proposition, that it must be lived forwards.'[2]

There comes a time when the healthiest thing to do is let go of the past and not let it define your future. For me, working to become a well-rounded, optimistic and emotionally stable woman, to be 'rooted' and to 'flow', as Virginia Woolf writes in the quote I opened this book with,[3] means taking ownership of my narrative and making a choice about the stories I tell about myself.

I choose not to be defined by the tragedies that have befallen my family. I choose to forgive my dad and be his friend. I choose not to come from a broken home but from a home that has changed and that grows. The death of people I love has made me grateful for the life I still get to live and the people I share it with. Losing a job that defined me made me redefine myself…These were not easy conclusions to come to, and then enact, in my daily life. I worked hard, emotionally, on myself – writing, going to therapy, talking, reading and listening to others share their stories. It is a privilege, though, to be able to choose a good life in this way. The challenges I have encountered have been surmountable thanks to my supportive family, my race, my education, my bank balance and so many other advantages that made it easier for me than others. If you are reading this as someone working from a very different foundation, you still have a power and potential to start making gentler choices for yourself, and see where that takes you.

There will inevitably be relatives you see more than others and are closer to. It's OK to invest more of your time and emotional energy into these people, in the same way a gentlewoman chooses to focus her efforts on friendships that are the most mutually fulfilling. You cannot be everything to everyone, particularly if you come from a sprawling family of step siblings, second cousins, and so on. Just make sure your expectations are aligned with your extended family's, because if you wish your cousins on your dad's side, for example, made more effort to get together with you then it is up to you to make that clear to them, and initiate the plans rather than seethe with resentment as you feel increasingly alienated. Gentlewomen take responsibility for setting in motion the life and relationships they want.

The idea of a 'nuclear family' has well and truly exploded. Mum, Dad, Brother, Sister – the old 2.4 ideal still exists but it's no longer what women are encouraged to aspire to with quite the same fervour. Instead, 'family' is up for grabs. Many of us find the stability and support others get from relatives from our friends or the community we identify with. In the brilliant documentary film *Paris is Burning*[4] about the drag ball scene in New York in the late 1980s, we see queer kids, many of whom are now homeless having been kicked out by homophobic parents, recreating a matriarchal paradigm with drag mothers presiding over their 'children' in big drag families which give them a strong sense of a shared identity. Your 'family' is what you make it because love runs thicker than blood.

Gay marriage is now legal in more than 70 countries, meaning the LGBTQ community can finally have their relationships validated by society in these places. In the UK, sperm and egg donation, surrogacy, adoption and fostering are becoming increasingly easy for us to access and build the families we want. My wife and I thought long and hard about how we would have children together. The fact that it wasn't just going to happen by chance forced us to have some very frank conversations about why we wanted a baby, which I think it would be beneficial for any couple, gay or straight, considering starting a family to have.

Family planning: a gentlewoman's suggested talking points

- Why is having a family important to you (maybe it isn't)?

- What's your timeline (if at all)?

- Picture yourself in 30 years' time – what will make you happy?

- What kind of parent do you imagine you'll be?

- What from your own upbringing would you emulate and what would you reject?

- What are your feelings about adoption and fostering? Under what circumstances would you consider these as options?

- Gay couples: what do you want from a donor? Friend or anonymous? Who will be the first to 'try'?

Gentlewomen are sensitive to other women's experiences, choices, hopes and losses and will not discuss their own journey to starting a family, or deciding not to, without careful consideration of their interlocutor's experience of this subject. We don't make assumptions, we listen, we ask questions and understand how loaded emotionally such conversations can be. I'm very happy to satisfy people's curiosity about how my wife and I decided on a donor and embarked on the process of having a child. But if someone is insensitive enough to ask which of us is the 'real mother' or be unduly interested in what they might call the 'father' but we call the 'donor' I quickly shut down. The language we use is so powerful – it has the potential to offend and exclude as much as soften or support. My friend Sophie Beresiner can't conceive as a result of breast cancer in her early thirties. After a period of attempting IVF she and her husband have begun the process of surrogacy with a donor egg. Sophie has a column about the trials and tribulations of her ongoing journey to motherhood in *The Times* newspaper[5] – at the time of writing her surrogate has yet to conceive. She tells me:

I'm a married straight woman approaching 40. I've got used to people assuming I have children or asking when we are going to 'try' – as if it's that easy! When I tell people that we are using a surrogate their facial expression readjusts as they process this information – it's as if I've blown their minds. The very worst thing people can say to us when I tell them about the pain, stress and financial burden of 'trying' is: 'Well, why don't you just adopt?' It's the thoughtless 'just' that is so painful. It implies that adoption is an easy solution for infertility. It sweeps our wants and needs under the carpet and even makes us feel guilty for it not being our first option. Such a question also suggests we haven't carefully considered all our options. My response, were I brave enough to say it, would be, 'Well, why don't you just adopt?'

Before starting any kind of chat with another woman about parenting, it is wise to think before you speak. If in doubt: just listen.

I find talking about my family with friends and hearing of their uniquely different experiences to be hugely helpful in providing a new perspective on my own. This is why I encourage you to get to know your friends' families, and introduce new partners to your own family as soon as you feel they might be a keeper. Inviting your partner and closest friends to family occasions is a great way of blending your life in this way.

Try to get together with your family (whoever *you* count as your family) as often as possible. Find things to celebrate, from birthdays to exam results or job promotions. You can guarantee you'll confront bad times together in life, so you must contrive enough good times to redress the balance.

Try taking your family out of their comfort zone when you spend time together as this can break embedded patterns of behaviour. If you always meet up at the same person's house and do the same kind of thing, you might find you end up having the same kind of fallings-out or frustrating conversations. Making the effort instead to go to a gallery, explore a new part of town or have lunch in a restaurant you've never been to can bring out the best in everyone and force your family to interact in the world as sophisticated people not as a 'pack' which permits long-standing ways of being with each other that, taken out of the confines of a home, suddenly seem less acceptable. As I've addressed throughout this book – yes, it may always feel like it's you initiating such plans and bringing people together. But welcome to being a gentlewoman. Simone de Beauvoir writes in her novel *All Men Are Mortal*: 'That's what I consider true generosity: You give your all, and yet you always feel as if it costs you nothing.'[6]

I really believe there are benefits to introducing your partner's or your closest friends' families to your own. It's tempting to put this off because you worry it could be awkward and a real social effort, involving you having to initiate conversations and connect the things (if any) they may have in common. But what's the worst that can happen if you just put them somewhere together and leave them to it? It is healthy to let go of the need to control such situations and the instinct to protect people from each other, particularly if you perceive their differences as insurmountable. Let the mess and the unpredictability in, because merging people with different life experiences so that they are forced to encounter diversity is soft power in action.

Try not to see the facets of your life as single pieces but instead as a completed puzzle, where friends, family, work, fun and everything in between fit together to make a whole. In the long run this will help you feel deep-rooted contentment even if it does cause some short-term challenges.

Have you ever found yourself going to great lengths to 'prove' to someone in your family you love them? Cooking elaborate meals, making something yourself it would have been easier to buy, arranging complicated outings. Sometimes showing a feeling in this way is easier than saying it. But at what emotional cost? 'Why am I doing this to myself?' is a question that could be asked of any of us, particularly at peak times of year such as Christmas, Hanukkah or Eid. Making an effort beyond what is expected is standard gentlewomanly behaviour, but think back to our approach to work and caring 'just more than enough'. There is a sweet spot that we should aim for in all our endeavours of believing something matters and doing our best, but not at the expense of everything else we care about, including ourselves. So if you find yourself weeping over *Love Actually* while hand-printing wrapping paper at 3am on Christmas Eve, ask yourself, Do I *need* to do this to show people I care? More important is being on top form for the big day so you can actually enjoy yourself and be the best daughter, sister, mother, partner you can be. When people knock themselves out to achieve an over-the-top version of whatever they're celebrating, I can't help thinking of poor Mrs Dalloway, who 'is always giving parties to cover the silence'. (There's more on how not to meet such a sorry end in the quest for perfection in Chapter 9.)

According to a YouGov survey,[7] the most likely trigger for an argument at the Christmas dinner table (and I'd imagine it's the same at any religious or cultural event that involves relatives reuniting), is, quite simply, 'family stuff'. Long-standing family tensions were responsible for 37 per cent of arguments, and sibling rivalries for 22 per cent, at Christmas in 2017. If you are the most emotionally stable and sorted of your friends and relatives, which is likely, then it will often fall to you to be the Switzerland of family fall-outs. But in the same way it is not your job to fix other people, it is not up to you to Ricki Lake every conflict. If you are always solving other people's problems, hearing one sister's side, then the other's, then saying, 'I think what Alice meant when she said, "Why did you have to marry such a dick?" was that she finds Paul's sense of humour challenging.' Or messaging your mum to say, 'Of course there was nothing wrong with telling Sarah she looks like she's "eating very well at the moment". You know she's just over sensitive', then quickly messaging Sarah to say, 'Honestly, Mum meant it as a compliment!!' And so on…they will stop bothering to find resolution themselves.

A gentlewoman's guide to avoiding family arguments

- Do not engage in complex emotional discussions over WhatsApp.
- Allow other people to think and feel what they need to without trying to take control.
- Talk openly and often with those you love.
- Avoid meeting in the places in which conflict has occurred in the past.
- Let others have the last word.
- Calmly remove yourself from discussions that are becoming aggressive or curdling.
- Don't be afraid to challenge bad behaviour or prejudice, but pick your battles wisely.
- Don't think another glass of wine at the dinner table when faced with family stress will make it better. It makes it worse.
- Try to think how/why the other person is acting the way they are.
- Don't overreact – remember to breathe and be empathetic.

Growing up, I had no idea that my mum and dad had issues in their relationship, they never raised their voices at each other, or me, and I was not an angry person. I don't think I once slammed a door or shouted at my parents in my entire teenagehood. I wasn't suppressing anything, I just had a good life and at that point had nothing to be hurt or frustrated about. I'm sure the day-to-day banter of bigger families is healthy and helps develop a thick skin that can set you up well for the harshness of today's world. But I do sometimes wonder if families *need* to argue as much as they do. Or if it is just a bad habit that a gentlewoman should seek to break by refusing to engage with people in an aggressive or unpleasant manner and hoping others follow suit.

Most arguments are never over the thing they are ostensibly about but are instead the manifestation of big, deep-seated issues that have never been adequately addressed. If conflict is really a problem in your family to the extent that it ruins any get-togethers, I'm afraid the only thing for it is to tackle the root cause. Resentment, guilt, jealousy – these are complex emotions that it takes time, honesty and communication to resolve. I'm not suggesting an intervention as such, but you could take responsibility for initiating one-to-one conversations with people, at the right time, and when you are clear on what you want to say and what you hope to achieve from each discussion, that begins to open up the possibility of bringing those unsaid things out into the light.

Empathy is what will help most in navigating family conflict with grace. We must always seek to understand how someone else's life experiences have shaped the way they act in situations. Even if you disagree with their position, being kind enough to understand it rather than instantly push against it can lead to the kind of resolution that will make your family life a lot happier.

Being better at communicating as a family will also help keep the peace. Perhaps suggest WhatsApp groups are just for exchanging pictures and salutations, making plans and sending each other links to articles. Big discussions should always be done in person if possible, or at least via a Skype call. It's a lot easier to misconstrue tone in a text message and people are prone to being more careless in the things they say and the way they say them when communicating via green speech bubbles. Someone on your 'Fam-a-lam' WhatsApp group could have taken offence at a joke and never replied, but how were you to know? Not being able to read cues of body language and eye contact can lead to small misunderstandings being blown out of proportion.

What we are trying to achieve isn't a linear process. Looking at the emotional arc of my adult life, which had been on an upwards trajectory for a while now, the birth of my daughter last summer took that steady line and made it as erratic as a seismograph just before an earthquake. Becoming a new parent stripped me of all but my basest sense of self. Six months in and I am able to start remembering the things beyond my baby that help make me *me*. But in the beginning it was the ultimate test of character. Five days after the birth we were back in hospital. We hadn't slept for a week and were still reeling from the labour and now there was something wrong with our daughter and no world existed except the one in that children's ward. I saw no further than the walk to and from the toilet in the low yellow light of the ward at night. We slept in a single camp bed somehow, together, with our baby next to us, inconceivably tiny in her big, blue hospital-issue cot. We forgot ourselves completely. In other words, self-care, diet, my appearance, friends, social media, work…none of the things

I normally drew on to help me live well and feel myself bore any relevance to the visceral moment I was in. Survival mode made the trappings of normal life meaningless. But, at the lowest point, Jen and I both found that we had a well of emotional resources to draw on, separately and together. The gentleness that I had nurtured in my deepest self became its most powerful. In the absence of everything but fear and love in a time of crisis, it was this more than 'toughness' that got us through. Our daughter got better in several days and we slowly readjusted to things being OK again, but that trauma taught me to trust in the woman I had become. And so when I think about the family my wife and daughter and I will evolve into as our roots spread and grow tangled with each others', I know that becoming, being and staying a gentlewoman is the greatest gift I can give them.

Gentle suggestions for being a family

- Keep an address book (or Google sheet) containing all your extended family's contact details.

- Send birthday cards even to relatives you rarely see as it shows they remain on your mind and it's more meaningful that you remember to send a card on their birthday than at Christmas.

- Invite your mum or dad to a party.

- Buy thoughtful gifts that show you 'get' them.

- If someone is struggling, for whatever reason, offer practical help – cook, clean, do grocery shopping. Even if they say it's not necessary it often is.

- Try not to only call or message when you need something.

- Share book, TV or film recommendations as a way of connecting.

- Try to listen to what people are really saying behind their words.

- Don't just fix your parents' or grandparents' issues with their computer or smartphone, have the patience to explain to them what they were doing wrong and empower them to know how to avoid the problem next time.

- Never stay quiet to keep the peace. If a family member says something that offends you, call them on it and calmly argue your alternative point of view. Don't be scared of healthy debate.

- Take the time to explain your job or passions to your family so they could accurately explain to someone else what you do or are into; avoid just saying 'I'm in finance' or 'I work in media'. Likewise, make the effort to understand your family's jobs and hobbies even if they are completely out of your frame of reference.

CHAPTER 9

Being online

...YOU have left the group.

If only it was possible to make a French exit from a WhatsApp group chat. Instead, the only way to extricate yourself is to effectively stand in the middle of a party and loudly exclaim, 'BORING! I'm off.'

It's no wonder we prefer to just let our phones ping with relentless banter and banalities rather than risk being considered rude. It's possible, of course, to mute group chats, but with a hierarchy of missives from urgent plans and serious business to cat gifs flying at us from every online orifice – WhatsApp, iMessage, Instagram, Messenger, Slack, Snapchat, to name but a few – it's easier to give up *trying* to control the noise and just let such constant tugs for attention overwhelm our phones and our senses.

We are all participating in an 'attention economy' where brands alongside the individuals in our networks are competing for our 'eyeballs' (as people are often referred to in the marketing industry) on their content. App designers use the psychology of gambling to win our interest, with the act of pulling down to refresh an inbox or news feed mirroring the way we would pull down the lever of a slot machine, tingling with anticipation as we wait to see our prize – more content! Be aware of this and be an active participator in the digital sphere. We cannot fight it, but we can as gentlewomen exercise as much autonomy as possible within it.

So if the fact that you are still being followed around the internet by the same pair of slippers you once googled really bothers you, take control of your digital life and disable cookies or change your preferences. To what extent do you personally feel that your data is a fair exchange for the free services you consume online? Be questioning and be conscious, it's a Wild West out there so saddle up and take the reins.

As advertisers battle for our attention, so do our friends and colleagues. Instant messaging has given rise to an endlessly stressful state of existence: being virtually tapped on the shoulder and told to look at this, answer that, respond, respond, respond to other people *on top* of whatever else you are doing, almost constantly throughout a day. And the more we are asked to engage with *everything* instantly the less likely we are to engage with *anything* meaningfully, even when it is actually important. This is no way to live.

We gentlewomen need time to think and space to be, and when something is important we want to give our response to it the care it deserves. So, how do we tackle the stress, strains and sensory overload that the digital deluge brings? First, we seek to remove as many unnecessary digital distractions from our day-to-day life as possible, while still remaining connected to, and emotionally available for, the people who need us most. Sounds simple *but* it involves reconfiguring quite a lot of your mind.

Take an audit of the messaging platforms you use and the chats you're signed up to and in the same way you might sort through the contents of your wardrobe, forcibly ask yourself:

Is this useful?

Does it make me feel good?

Do I need it in my life?

Is it taking up too much space?

Muting a chat for a year is like putting a stack of old T-shirts you know you'll never wear but aren't brave enough to throw out in the bottom of a drawer. You'll always know they are there, taking up room. I find the line 'I'm leaving this group but please do message me separately if anything's urgent' the most straightforward and courteous way to break up with a group chat. While Kate Moss's famous adage, 'never explain', doesn't hold much sway for a gentlewoman this is one of the few occasions it can be useful.

You might also consider turning off 'last seen' on WhatsApp (settings – account – privacy) to remove the pressure to reply when you know that they know that you have read their message. Alternatively, ditch all other instant-messaging apps from your phone entirely and just text. Communicating via a single platform is perfectly acceptable, and in pursuit of a calmer, more streamlined life, it really is preferable.

As you detox your own digital communications, spare a thought for others and the necessity or timing of your notes to them too. There are no rules about what we can send and when (nude pics aside) and we're all so used to our friends and family sporadically popping up on our phones, we just accept this as a new normal. But it is in fact quite thoughtless to send funny gifs that require a response in the middle of the day to someone who you know has a demanding job, or to involve a friend with a young baby in complicated arrangements over text in the early evening when they probably have their hands full doing bedtime. It's good practice to give yourself a second to think before you send. And try to fit your needs into their lives. To put it another way, would you call them or ring their doorbell at any hour? Practise this caution when it comes to messaging.

It won't be long before emails become obsolete and seem as cumbersome as the fax machine. Who knows how we'll be communicating professionally and sharing information in decades to come – perhaps we'll just be downloading our thoughts directly. But rather than worry what the future holds, let's focus on mastering the medium of the email first. Because if we aren't kinder to ourselves in the pursuit of inbox perfection and take back some control, we'll fast become the exhausted victims rather than astute users of digital comms.

A gentlewoman's approach to email

- Don't email someone in the same office as you if you could walk over and ask the question in person.
- If you are taking a holiday and turning on 'out of office' don't then send mixed messages by checking and replying to emails every day. Switch off and trust that everything can wait (if it can't, you'll know about it).
- Never write comedy out-of-office messages. Keep it simple and factual.
- Be mindful of who you cc – or don't – in emails. Never use 'cc'

as a way of 'telling on' someone and never deliberately exclude a colleague.

- When addressing someone or cc'ing, do not send or cc in hierarchy of importance, always alphabetize when you cc.
- Avoid 'all company' emails unless truly necessary. Even if you think something is *hilarious*, don't assume all 374 of your fellow employees will too.
- If you find yourself writing an email that starts, 'has anyone taken my mug/stapler/mouse?' delete it immediately.
- Block out time in the day to answer emails – first thing in the morning, after lunch and then around 4pm work well. Haphazardly refreshing and replying to new messages throughout the day makes it impossible to focus on any one task. Also it makes you feel constantly available.
- Don't expect a response straight away from anyone. Think of the other person's workload as well as your own and avoid sending 'chaser' emails unless really necessary.
- Unsubscribe to anything that clutters your email.
- It's OK to email out of hours but don't expect a response. Likewise, avoid responding to work emails sent out of hours or it sets a precedent.
- If an empty inbox makes you feel on top of things, just be mindful of when 'perfectish' is better than perfect. Even if your inbox is bursting with red flags, leaving the office on time, seeing to the task 'objectively' the next day, or incrementally over a few days, may be a healthier and more balanced approach.
- Don't be a slave to your emails. Remember replying and fielding emails probably isn't in your job description and allows for very little creative endeavour.

- Convey your own voice in emails. Trying to be overly polite can read as obsequiousness, but being too brief can be misconstrued as bluntness. Aim for brief and engaging.
- Ban truisms or acronyms, particularly EOP, CLOP or any variation of 'end of the day'.
- Avoid 'just' in an email if used to indicate the reason behind your sending: 'I just wanted to drop you a note...' It comes across as apologetic and you should be confident in the importance of your note.
- Always check you have spelled people's names correctly.
- If compelled to end a serious email with a couple of kisses ('xx'), ask yourself why? Are you trying to sound less demanding, worried you'll come across as bossy otherwise? If this is the case I want a Keynote presentation on the impact of third-wave feminism on workplace culture by CLOP.

The late Nora Ephron, who wrote the movie *You've Got Mail*,[1] a love letter to emailing if ever there was one, was so taken with the medium she wrote a piece for *The New York Times* in 2007 entitled, 'The Six Stages of E-Mail'. In it she celebrates the freedoms that the then relatively new form afforded:

> *And it saves so much time. It takes five seconds to accomplish in an e-mail message something that takes five minutes on the telephone. The phone requires you to converse, to say things like hello and goodbye, to pretend to some semblance of interest in the person on the other end of the line. Worst of all, the phone occasionally forces you to make actual plans with the people*

*you talk to – to suggest lunch or dinner – even if you have no
desire whatsoever to see them. No danger of that with e-mail.*[2]

Some people love writing long, descriptive accounts of their
life. But emailing such a weighty piece of prose sends with it a heavy
expectation of a response. To certain friends that's stressful and
intimidating, and maybe that's why they haven't got back to you at
all. Others will relish a long read, and some might prefer a call or
even a quick back-and-forth on text. Think about the person you
are corresponding with and measure the form and content of your
correspondence to suit them as much as yourself.

I have increasingly found myself communicating via email with
friends who live abroad when actually a phone call or Skype chat
would be a more meaningful way of connecting. If you want to make
a long-distance friendship work it's important to be in touch at least
every other month, beyond liking each other's Instagram pics.

I like the idea of seeing to your social correspondence as people
did in the era of the aforementioned *The English Gentlewoman*: 'In
your correspondence aim at those qualities which are most valuable
in conversation: simplicity, readiness, truth'. It goes on:

> *How many minds 'cream and mantle' from the want of energy
> to pour themselves out in words; on the other hand, how some,
> equally well intentioned, drown their very senses in their
> torrent of remarks, which dashes like a waterfall into a somber
> pool of ennui below!*

Next time you spend ten minutes scrolling through Twitter
or Instagram comments, be conscious of 'drowning your senses
in a torrent of remarks'. I can only imagine what the original

gentlewomen would have made of today's hashtags and cat emojis.

A gentlewoman should put as much care into the way she communicates online as she does offline, because a slapdash, speak-now-think-later approach to engaging with the conversations both personal and political that constantly spin around us will breed stress, anxiety, aggression and unkindness. I'm not saying we shouldn't engage with the necessary debates and discussions of our time, but I advocate that we all need to take a breath and think before we type. Our digital footprint is now more permanent than ever.

Almost a year into my new job in advertising, I received via Twitter some vitriol from one of the industry's most well-respected 'gurus'. He had taken against a piece I had written for a newspaper about my move from being a magazine editor to a creative director in an agency. He didn't like my 'tone' or the fact that I had been offered a senior role in an industry I'd no experience of, despite my having explained in the piece that it was my boss's desire to bring different and new thinking (and my 15 years' editorial experience) into the business that had led to my appointment in the first place. I'd have been open to engaging with his argument if it wasn't for the fact that he then tweeted: 'I bet her mum has her ideas pinned up on her fridge with little fridge magnets.'

I found it troubling for a number of reasons. Most importantly because this highly regarded writer and thinker was so determined to infantilize a successful woman and her 'ideas', but also the insinuation that my mum is a user of fridge magnets, because for the record she finds them quite naff. There were further disappointing comments from other, mainly male, ad landers: 'sounds like she's been hired to churn out female friendly content…' wrote one blue-ticked 'ledge', because God forbid a woman would be capable of anything else. Sigh. On the scale of online abuse that women, particularly those in the public eye, receive, this barely registers. But it is an example of the kind of everyday sexism gentlewomen must continue to challenge.

When I read the first tweets from this unpleasant man and his Twitter friends I began composing my take-down – I could have turned this into a very public debate about the lack of diversity in the industry and the disconnect between certain creative leaders who liked to talk about 'change' and 'disruption' but weren't able to cope with the reality of it (me) – particularly when that reality meant listening to voices other than their own. But I didn't respond that night. I turned off my phone and went to bed. The next day I sent him an email:

> *I'm sorry you took such offence to a piece I wrote earlier this year. I can't say I enjoyed perusing your – and your friends' – comments about it on Twitter, particularly the one referring to my mother. Seemed quite unnecessarily unkind 'banter' from someone such as yourself. Perhaps you might like to meet in person and you can talk through your issues with me face to face? How about a coffee?*
>
> *Best regards*
> *Lotte*

Soft power is not about shouting the loudest or having the quickest, wittiest putdown, but rather considering the most effective way to change someone's mind. In this case, I knew my adversary would have relished getting into a Twitter fight and it would have quickly become a tit-for-tat contest of bravado. Would such a personality ever meaningfully engage with my points on this kind of a platform and deign to admit, 'Actually I was wrong. I'm sorry I cussed your mum. I'm a 70-year-old man, that was pathetic of me'? Of course not! Deploying soft power at times like this, means stating your objections in a reasonable and clear way, not using aggressive language or threats, and allowing opportunities to listen to an opposing point of view (even if you do end up quickly rejecting it).

In this instance, I knew it would be more powerful and more effective if I responded as a gentlewoman and suggested a real-world conversation, when perhaps we might meet as fellow humans and discover common ground. Alas, he ignored my invitation but sent me back an essay, the gist of which was that I had taken the job of a creative director from someone more deserving because they had worked their way up in the industry for years and would now be 'in their forties or fifties with a family to support'. As a 37-year-old woman who had worked her way up, albeit in a different industry, over a number of years and who also had a family to support, I couldn't help but read between the lines and wonder if he would have been so affronted by my change in career had I been a man.

Taking control of things that happen to us, and turning them into stories that *we* tell, in our own voice, in our own way, is the source of power behind movements such as Me Too and Black Lives Matter. You don't need to be a journalist or celebrity to do this, we all have the potential to construct our narratives and share them with the world. Never forget the power of your own honesty in this respect. As soon as I shared the account of my interactions with this much-revered advertising 'maverick', my DMs were flooded with messages of support and people sharing similar stories with me. I had created a conversation and raised a number of issues without engaging on his terms.

In such circumstances, if someone treats you unfairly at work or unjustifiably takes against you on social media, I believe there are always three options.

1. **Don't engage**

   Has its place but you must ask yourself what ignoring something that has hurt you will do for your self-respect. Silence can be a weapon in itself, and if that is your modus operandi for a particular reason I trust that you have other ways to express yourself.

2. **Go hard (softly)**

   If 'going hard' is your attitude it is easier for debates to become personal and for humour to veer into meanness. Soft power can be as effective as hard aggression and is ultimately more nurturing of yourself than gearing yourself up for a fight and wasting unnecessary energy on anger and negativity. However unfairly a person has behaved, matching their actions only does a disservice to yourself.

3. **Keep it classy**

   Self-edit. Seek the point of view of others you trust before engaging and be the better person. This may be manifest in any number of ways given the multitude of attacks one can face in the digital space, but it essentially comes down to what queen of gentlewomen Michelle Obama said when she delivered her speech at the Democratic Convention in 2016: 'When they go low, we go high.'

Key to your decision about how to respond to a person or issue that affects you on social media is giving yourself the time you need to think. Compose a response, but save it and come back to it after an hour or so. Don't throw your unthought-through missives into the digital savannah without first considering the consequences of them.

Be shrewd in the content you share online. 'Why would anyone care' is a question all good newspaper or magazine editors ask of the ideas that they are pitched. We gentlewomen are the editors of our own lives, choosing to associate with the people, ideas and experiences which best reflect our sense of identity just as a publication with a point of view must. This craft of curating, of choosing *this* not this, and knowing instinctively why, is essential to ensure your online output does not negate the work you have done on yourself in the real world to be a woman of character. Before posting, commenting or sharing, ask what an editor would of any words or images presented to her – 'Is this useful, funny, informative or entertaining?' 'Why this and why now and what's our unique take on it?' As legendary editor of *Vanity Fair* Tina Brown wrote in her *Diaries*: 'A magazine – a relevant one – should be a sound not an echo.'[3]

Our aim is that our online self best aligns with our offline one, which is integral if we believe a 'joined-up' life is at the root of real contentment. But it's easy for a social-media persona to become the Hyde to our Jekyll as mediums such as Instagram seduce us into avarice and showing off, while Twitter nudges us into pontificating or having an opinion for the sake of opining. We might soon find ourselves expressing ourselves in a way or saying certain things we never would in real life. But as the good doctor in Robert Louis Stevenson's novel eventually realizes: '… of the two natures that contended in the field of my consciousness, even if I could rightly be said to be either, it was only because I was radically both.'[4]

We are 'radically both' our online and our offline selves. Employing all those same qualities that make you a gentlewoman in the real world in your online endeavours makes it more possible to act with authenticity in this space. Of course we may 'edit' our online self as we construct it, posting only the most flattering selfies, sharing only the good news, but it is the manner in which we do this that matters.

A gentlewoman's rules of engagement

- Don't say anything to anyone you wouldn't say if you met them in person.
- Be kind, be thoughtful.
- Spend your time supporting the people doing positive things for the causes you believe in.
- Don't lie or exaggerate.
- Be generous.
- Remember not all thoughts need to be said.
- Be aware you leave a trace and a record.
- Don't follow the flock. Be your own #inspo.

The pressure (perceived or otherwise) to have something to offer every possible social media outlet can leave us feeling spent; we must engage people with careful wordplay, deploy a thoughtful voice on the political agenda, upload unique content while also showcasing our carefully curated, tasteful existence and passions. It is time to employ the old saying, that it is better to do one thing really well, than to spread yourself thinly. A gentlewoman wants to be a forerunner not a chaser and this involves having the gumption to be selective about where your voice feels most at home...Is it with sassy Snapchat filters, is it serious hard-hitting Twitter thought or is it niche Pinterest collections? Try focusing on one platform and really honing your presence there.

When I consider which of my social apps spark joy, I would have deleted Facebook a long time ago because it is rife with negativity; from the shocking fake news articles that are shared to the endless posts moaning about everything from BREXIT to breakfast cereal. But it has become a kind of mausoleum of my past. When I have the time I intend to download everything precious to my computer and delete my account entirely, but until then I have removed it from my phone, abandoned Messenger and not once felt that I'm missing out on anything.

Twitter is too shouty for me. I enjoy scrolling but I rarely engage as I don't like the pressure to perform my opinions so loudly or be consistently 'banterific'. I'm aware that I don't use the platform to its fullest potential; I tweet customer service departments of organizations I wish to complain to – Sky Broadband has had more Twitter engagement from me than anyone else – ever. And I share links to things I have written with little in the way of commentary. I am a happy voyeur and have been careful to curate the people I follow to expose me to a diversity of voices, but I know I could be joining conversations in a far more meaningful way.

Twitter tips from an activist

Gina Martin (@ginamartin_uk) is an activist/writer who successfully campaigned to make 'upskirting' illegal in the UK.

If you are about to start using Twitter for the first time with a particular aim in mind – promoting a cause, finding work, campaigning, etc. – where should you start?
Fill your feed with people with whom there is an intersection, whether you are an artist or you are an educator or you care about kids or whatever: you will find every person in the world who is in any industry on there. So, follow all of those people. When I was starting out with my campaign to make 'upskirting' a criminal offence I did this, and then I found their contact details and reached out to those people through another medium – email, or even handwritten letters. I started to make connections offline. I think we so often see one platform as the be all and end all, and actually it is just a tool in the arsenal. Once I had made a connection with people in real life I started connecting with them publicly on Twitter, asking them to talk about and support my work in the same way that I was doing for them. You can retweet until the cows come home. But like everything you have to make a genuine connection.

How can we make our voices heard among all of the noise on Twitter?
The biggest rule with social media is consistency. Limit what you talk about on the platform to three or four things; for me these are human rights, feminism, equality issues and the power of positivity and creativity. I follow people in these worlds, I talk about

these subjects, I get involved in the community. Consistency is key because when people come to your channel or when they see you on a feed, they want to know what to expect. If you are constantly posting about different things, they don't know what to come to you for.

What are your personal rules for using Twitter?
I try to think before I tweet anything. I save it in my drafts and then come back to it. The reactiveness of Twitter can create fire storms with people and arguments and debates. The main rule for Twitter has to be: Do I need to say this right now, and am I the person to say it?

Instagram is where I feel most at home. To me it is a safe space which even when being used to highlight injustice by people tends to encourage action and support more than negativity. It feels positive and uplifting and, most importantly, kind, which is what leads me to think it intrinsically the most gentlewomanly of social media to participate in.

Stories is a great outlet for our more playful side, while the main feed is a place to express ourselves authentically and share experiences. When I found out I didn't get the job as editor in chief of *ELLE*, I knew people would be talking about it and speculating over how I was feeling and what I'd do next so I decided to be the author of my own story, and be open about what had happened and how I felt. I posted a striking image of a model backstage at a fashion show flexing her muscles and wrote:

When someone tells me they are a very private person, I want to ask why. Being unduly guarded about yourself can make it harder to connect with other people and suggests that there is something holding you back from inhabiting your most authentic self in public. In the social dance that takes place when we first begin forging a meaningful relationship with someone new, there is a give and take of information. Unless you start to reveal how you *feel* about the facts you are providing, your conversation will soon lose momentum and remain in the realm of boring small talk. Online there are, of course, valid safety concerns that motivate privacy and I would never suggest you are as open publicly as you would be with someone you were talking to over a drink in a bar. But it is an interesting modern conundrum: how much of your true thoughts and feelings should you reveal online in order to be your most authentic self, and how much makes you vulnerable and at risk of everything from trolling to hacking? Being a gentlewoman means handling this delicate balance with care. If we return to the idea of being the editor of our online selves then employing that editorial 'filter' is a good way of recognizing when truthfulness has veered into TMI or when silence stands for a fear of vulnerability.

It is gentlewomanly to seek permission from anyone else you are involving in your content before posting it. But at the same time, don't try to police someone else's social media – the instant nature of the medium means that asking permission isn't always possible, and people will make mistakes. Being too precious can lead to unnecessary stress. When it comes to portraying your children on social media, however, you might want to create some boundaries. I spoke to my former boss Lorraine Candy about why she hadn't shown her children's faces online until recently, and what the decision to do so has meant for their family dynamic.

Meet a gentlewoman

Lorraine Candy was my boss at *ELLE*. She is now Luxury Content Director of the *Sunday Times*, Editor-in-Chief of *Style*, and writes a hugely popular column about being the mother of teens.

When and why did you decide to start showing your kids' images on social media after hiding them from the camera for so long?

I was conscious of, and learning about, their growing digital footprint when I decided it was OK to do this occasionally and with permission. Having had a weekly family column in a national newspaper for almost six years covering them as younger children where I masked their identity and wrote 'out of sync' with events to make them unfollowable, as it were, I wanted to be able to give them a presence as they got older. I am a journalist specializing in family and teenagers when I write, so it seems a little hypocritical not to include the children when they are happy to be included and always with their OK. They approve anything I write before I post on any social platform and approve all pictures. It's a personal decision and very much up to the individual. I didn't think it right to chronicle their life in detail as some parents do online but more to refer to them when relevant. I rarely put the teens on Facebook though as they don't agree with Facebook because it isn't 'cool' apparently. And I don't think I have put more than two pictures of my son up as he is less keen.

What are your personal rules for posting pics of or comments about your kids?

I ask their permission, show them the post with words and pictures and then if they are happy I do it. If they come back later and want it taken down I always do. That has happened a couple of times when a friend has maybe teased them. My youngest is seven – she understands social media as we have explained it and explored it with her and she has watched her older siblings on it. Parents need to sit down with children and talk it through, look at the sites with them and discuss the dangers as well. I don't have access to my teens' phones but I do ask that they show me their social feeds and who they follow if I have a real and practical worry about something, which they do.

What advice would you give mothers of new babies about their approach to sharing their child's life online?
When I interviewed child psychologist Steve Biddulph I took a step back and reviewed my opinion. He believes we should never post pictures of our children because even if we have consent, do our children really understand the possible effects of the picture living for ever in their digital history? But personally I felt that was going too far in our changing modern world. We are the first generation of parents to live with this. There is a joy in family life which is good to share, a joy in being a working mum and being honest about that and what it takes, so I do think spreading the positive side of parenting through images is a good thing. It's a balance and one should constantly review the situation as media develop.

What are social media refuseniks really scared of? I have one female friend, who has never engaged with a single social media platform. She's a very sociable person and has a job arranging events that she wants other people to share online. So why has she not been tempted on to a platform, even as a voyeur? She told me: 'If I go on holiday, or get a new job, or have a baby – I want to tell my friends about it in person so I can have a genuine connection with them about it and see the look on their faces when I tell them. If you're following all your friends on social media you can know everything about their lives without even having a phone conversation with them.'

In some ways, not muddying yourself in the world of social media at all could be considered the ultimate gentlewomanly move. To be so confident in yourself and so content with real life is everything we have been working towards in the past nine chapters. But herein lies the most prescient point about being a modern gentlewoman: it is our relationship with others and with the social milieu in which we live that differentiates our way of being from the crowd's. If we refuse to use these platforms merely as a mirror, to obsessively track the number of double taps our latest selfie has achieved, but instead we reflect our best self outwards into the world in order to forge connections with other people different to ourselves, listen to their stories and hope that ours can resonate with or inspire people we don't even know, then our digital lives take on a real *raison d'être*.

Not engaging at all in social media may mean you find your finger drifting further and further from the pulse. It is important to be in the fray but not controlled by it. We should not be myopic but know and care about what is happening in the world of politics or popular culture around us. Curate a world view and then seek to open it out so you aren't refracting only what you want to see from the world in your digital prism. I read a newspaper every day. An actual printed copy, not an app. I find this the best way to 'hack' the algorithm that feeds me the news and views it thinks I will like, keeping me locked in my personal echo chamber. Scanning the spreads of newspapers with different political agendas enables me to decide for myself what I want to read and I often find myself engaging with stories that are far out of my frame of reference and yet tell me something new or challenge me in a way I'm glad of.

A gentlewoman's media 'diet' should be wide-ranging, high and low and eclectic. Surround yourself with a diversity of thought, both in print and online, so that you are aware of the issues that matter to other people. This will keep you current and conscious of the lens you view the world through, which in turn makes you a far more interesting and socially agile person. Broaden your horizons and as well as taking an audit of all the people you follow on social media consume content from high as well as low sources, read as much as you can from as many perspectives as you can and this will make you a well-rounded person.

How do we continue to consume people's perfect pictures of their ostensibly perfect lives without it leading to feelings of jealousy in even the most mature and well-balanced woman? And why does social media have this *Freaky Friday*ish power to turn us all back into insecure teenagers? Being a gentlewoman means being secure enough in yourself to let the posturing and preposterousness of other people wash over you like a rolling wave laps the sand. Or if you really don't like the way someone's posts are making you feel – consciously unfollow. In the same way in Chapter 5 we looked at the importance of surrounding yourself with friends who bring out your best, uplift and inspire you, when it comes to who you choose to populate your social media feeds with – you have the power to curate this portfolio.

You can control how you 'show up' on social media, and approach your presence with gentleness. Don't ever feel that you can't revel in your own happiness or success as you are worried it'll make other people feel 'less than'. All you can do is be conscious of your tone and of the social context of your words or images and act with authenticity.

Sometimes we are so busy curating our tastes, we forget to taste the world around us; we need to allow our senses to feel, smell and see, rather than filter, edit and frame. We need a true connection with the life we live rather than the version of our life we offer up. Inhabit your world before exhibiting it.

Gentlewomen appreciate aesthetics and take care over the words and pictures they post so that they exude the same quality and sophistication as everything in their life does. This means Instagram posts have some visual value and that captions and tweets are written well and spelled correctly. But this is not about seeking perfection, rather keeping one's social media output in line with how you want to present your view of the world.

In her 1977 book *On Photography*, Susan Sontag muses on emotional detachment and the image. She writes: 'A way of certifying experience, taking photographs is also a way of refusing it – by limiting experience to a search for the photogenic, by converting experience into an image, a souvenir. Travel becomes a strategy for accumulating photographs.'[5]

Do we now travel, eat in restaurants, go for riverside walks, visit art galleries just so we can capture the experience in a 1080 x 1080px square? Sontag argues: 'Photographs are a way of imprisoning reality...One can't possess reality, one can possess images – one can't possess the present but one can possess the past.'

It is when we risk caring more about 'imprisoning' reality than participating in it that a gentlewoman stops to think about her priorities. It is easier to control your online image than it is to control the way you are perceived in the flesh and it is tempting to 'edit' your face so your skin is unblemished (and have you really grown cute little puppy ears?). But real joy and real love exist on the fleshy, blemished, wrinkled and unfiltered side of the screen. This is the side that can't be contained or filtered, but spills out of the frame with its messy and unpredictable humanity. It might not look as pretty or perfect, but it's certainly a more fulfilling place to be.

Social media should be a happy addition to a life well lived, not the extent of it. If you find yourself constantly checking your posts to see how many likes or retweets you have got, you must confront the real motivation for sharing them in the first place. You don't need to seek others' agreement with how you live your life – share it so that you have presence and are engaged but you shouldn't need to ask for validation; a gentlewoman has enough self-assurance to validate herself. So turn off notifications on your phone, post something because it is beautiful or meaningful to you and if it resonates with others that's a bonus.

Instagram tips from an artist and influencer

Jessi Raulet, aka @EttaVee, is an artist, designer and social media influencer who has become well known for her hand-painted, bright and bold designs. Here she shares her top tips for getting the most from the platform.

- Ask yourself: 'Am I adding value to those who are following me?' Understand what people are looking for and listen to what they want.

- Make your posts consistent in terms of lighting. For example, I shoot all of my pictures using daylight so they visually look cohesive in my Instagram grid.

- Interact with followers. I try to respond to as many comments and DMs as I can, even if it's just to say, 'Hey, thanks.' When I'm writing captions I really try to engage people and ask them questions to encourage them to comment. I have them in mind whenever I am posting.

- Try not to post more than twice a day, because what I found is that the less that I post for the sake of posting, the more time I have to create better and more meaningful content. Quality over quantity.

- Create a community. I am connecting with other artists and women of colour, and it is just really cool to see that we are all out here building our dreams together, and it is great to have that support from each other. Collaborating on projects within your community can also help get your work seen by new people.

- Have your own 'filter' for what you post. My criteria is that everything needs to fit within my brand category, so it should be colourful, uplifting, fun, unexpected.

- Be authentic and play to your strengths. I know that I am really good with colour, and so that is something that I have brought into my art and into my Instagram persona. I am also really good at connecting with people in person, so I wanted to bring that aspect of myself as well by being very open and inviting.

- Keep it real. I won't try to pretend to be happy if I am not at that moment, I probably just won't post anything.
- Coherence is important because it communicates quickly what you are about. So if someone is to open my page, they get it right away: Joyful Colour. If you are a business, for example, or an artist who needs to promote themselves, your grid is a quick way to pitch yourself without saying anything because it evokes a *feeling and vibe*.

What is a gentlewoman to make of the fact that more than 250 people around the world have died taking selfies since 2011?[6] Are we really so narcissistic now that we put the pursuit of our own image over our personal safety, or has the prevalence of performing life online made us feel invincible and immune to the dangerous realities of, say, hanging off a moving jet ski to get that perfect wind-in-the-hair shot? I would suggest that a gentlewoman posts selfies sparingly, and when she does they should capture authentically lived moments that show her really smiling because she is actually happy, and the self-portrait is not the result of an hour spent in her bathroom fiddling with the lighting, the angles and then twitching her lips into the most flattering half-pout before face-tuning herself into someone resembling a living doll more than an actual human woman. Instagram Stories or Snapchat are mediums better suited for those 'here's me…' moments. And when a gentlewoman does post a selfie, she avoids attributing any deeper meaning to it. 'Just sitting here, looking totes gawgeous drinking a flat white and contemplating the injustice of life in Yemen right now' or similar smacks of inauthenticity.

You have the power to redefine what is meant by 'influence' in the digital world. By acting with kindness, carefulness and empathy, taking time to think and to craft your online self so that it is a seamless extension of the 'real' you, there is an opportunity to truly influence others through soft power.

At my lowest point I longed to escape reality because being in it reminded me of all that I had lost and it made me feel things like sadness and anger. But there was no fantasy universe where everything would be perfect, there never really is. There is only *this*, and there is only me. I would have to gently allow the pain in and then channel it into something just as real but ultimately more fulfilling. By questioning my behaviour and challenging my deepest ways of thinking I began to build myself up again from a new, more stable base. I considered the relationships in my life I most wanted to nurture and worked towards becoming a good and positive influence on those people as much as on myself. I allowed myself to grow and to figure out how I defined happiness. I looked inwards and then I looked up and out. I realized that reality wasn't a scary place any more, it was where I could find love, success and the deep contentment of a joined-up life and then siphon the energy that came from such an honest place into everything I did: the clothes I wore, the work I chose, the parties I hosted and the stories I told on social media.

Plato's Cave might sound like the latest dodgy influencer-endorsed festival in Tulum. But it is in fact a fascinating ancient allegory that tells the story of prisoners chained up in a cave, unable to turn their heads. All they can see is the wall of the cave, they don't realize that behind them burns a fire and between the fire and the prisoners there is a parapet, along which people hold up objects that cast shadows on the wall of the cave. The prisoners have only ever heard the echoes and seen the shadows cast by the objects. When they are released, they finally turn their heads and see for the first time the *real* objects which have created the 'versions' in which they have mistakenly invested truth and meaning.[7]

I can't help but feel that unless we take gentle care amid the brutal pressures of modern life, we are in danger of becoming prisoners in this cave, unable to distinguish reality from the images we are relentlessly bombarded with of what it is to be a happy and successful woman today.

Don't settle for a shadow of yourself, a flickering and insubstantial idea of the person you could become. Escape the shackles holding you back, turn your head and face the fire. You have never known freedom like it.

Gentle suggestions for being online

- Regularly edit the people you follow.
- Use hashtags sparingly.
- Post a maximum of one selfie per six squares.
- Switch your phone off at night.
- Swap news apps for newspapers.
- Be tolerant of other people's online foibles.
- Question news.
- Avoid enacting the memes everyone else is (there are better ways to feel part of something).
- Use spell check.
- Strive for naturalness in your pictures.
- Experience life first and capture it later.

BIBLIOGRAPHY

INTRODUCTION

[1] Woolf, Virginia, *The Waves* (Vintage Classics, 2016)

[2] Anon., *The English Gentlewoman: A Practical Manual for Young Ladies on Their Entry into Society* (London, Henry Colburn, 1845)

[3] Nye, Joseph, *Bound to Lead: The Changing Nature of American Power* (Basic Books, 1990)

[4] Baudrillard, Jean, *Simulacra and Simulation* (University of Michigan Press, 1994)

CHAPTER 1: BEING AT HOME

[1] Capote, Truman, *Breakfast at Tiffany's* (Penguin Classics, 2000)

[2] Woolf, Virginia, *A Room of One's Own* (Penguin Modern Classics, 2002)

[3] Hublin, J. J., Ben-Ncer, A., Bailey, S. E., Freidline, S. E., Neubauer, S., Skinner, M. M., Bergmann, I., Le Cabec, A., Benazzi, S., Harvati, K. and Gunz, P., *New fossils from Jebel Irhoud, Morocco and the pan-African origin of Homo sapiens*, 546, 289–292 (*Nature*, 2017)

[4] Goring-Morris, A.N., Belfer-Cohen, A., 'A Roof Over One's Head: Developments in Near Eastern Residential Architecture

Across the Epipalaeolithic–Neolithic Transition', Bocquet-Appel, J.P., Bar-Yosef, O. (eds), *The Neolithic Demographic Transition and its Consequences* (Springer, Dordrecht, 2008)

[5] Renfrew, C., Bahn, P., *Archaeology: Theories, Methods and Practice* (Thames & Hudson, Seventh Edition, 2016)

[6] Duru, G., 'Sedentism and Solitude: Exploring the Impact of Private Space on Social Cohesion in the Neolithic', *Religion, History, and Place in the Origin of Settled Life*, edited by Hodder, I., pp. 162–185 (University Press of Colorado, 2018)

[7] Floss, H., *The Oldest Portable Art: the Aurignacian Ivory Figurines from the Swabian Jura (Southwest Germany)* (Palethnologie, [En ligne], 7 | 2015); https://journals.openedition.org/palethnologie/888

[8] Aubert, M., Setiawan, P., Oktaviana, A. A., Brumm, A., Sulistyarto, P. H., Saptomo, E. W., ... Brand, H. E. A., *Palaeolithic cave art in Borneo*, 564(7735), 254–257 (*Nature*, 2018); https://doi:10.1038/s41586-018-0679-9

[9] Clarke, J., *Decorating the Neolithic: An Evaluation of the Use of Plaster in the Enhancement of Daily Life in the Middle Pre-pottery Neolithic B of the Southern Levant*, 22(2), 177–186 (*Cambridge Archaeological Journal*, June 2012); https://doi:10.1017/S0959774312000224

[10] Demay, Laëtitia, Péan, Stéphane, Patou-Mathis, Marylène, *Mammoths used as food and building resources by Neanderthals: Zooarchaeological study applied to layer 4, Molodova I (Ukraine)*, Volumes 276–277 (*Quaternary International*, 2012); https://doi.org/10.1016/j.quaint.2011.11.019

[11] Bachelard, Gaston, *The Poetics of Space* (Penguin Classics, 2014)

CHAPTER 2: BEING A FRIEND

[1] Jennings, Elizabeth, 'Friendship', *New Collected Poems* (Carcanet Press, 2002)

[2] Nin, Anaïs, *The Diary of Anaïs Nin*, 1939–1944, Vol. 3

[3] Larkin, Philip, *Letters to Monica* (Faber & Faber, 2010)

[4] Donne, John, *No Man is an Island* (Souvenir Press, New Ed edition, 1988)

[5] Aristotle, *The Nicomachean Ethics*, translation: Adam Beresford (Penguin Classics, 2016)

[6] Dunbar, Robin, *How Many Friends Does One Person Need?: Dunbar's Number and Other Evolutionary Quirks* (Faber & Faber, 2011)

CHAPTER 3: BEING ALONE

[1] Laing, Olivia, *The Lonely City: Adventures in the Art of Being Alone* (Canongate Books, 2017)

[2] Hot Chip, 'Ready for the Floor'

[3] Freud, Sigmund, *The Psychopathology of Everyday Life* (Penguin Classics, New Ed edition, 2002)

[4] Marsh, Stephanie, 'The slow, steady rise of "conscious movement"' (*Guardian*, 2 October 2018), https://www.theguardian.com/life andstyle/2018/oct/02/the-slow-steady-rise-of-conscious-movement

[5] *RuPaul's Drag Race* (reality competition TV series)

CHAPTER 4: BEING SOCIABLE

[1] de Beauvoir, Simone, *The Second Sex* (Vintage Classics, 1977)

[2] Grosz, Stephen, *The Examined Life* (Vintage, 2014)

[3] Dunbar, Robin, 'Why drink is the secret to humanity's success', the *Financial Times*, 10 August 2018, https://www.ft.com/content/ c5ce0834-9a64-11e8-9702-5946bae86e6d

CHAPTER 5: BEING TOGETHER

[1] Gill, Alexandra, Marry Yourself Vancouver, http://4everluv.com/marry-yourself-services/

[2] YouGov survey, 'Does Anyone Believe in Marriage Anymore?', 28 June 2018, https://yougov.co.uk/topics/lifestyle/articles-reports/2018/06/28/does-anyone-believe-marriage-anymore

[3] Traister, Rebecca, 'Single Women Are Now the Most Potent Political Force in America', *New York Magazine*, 21 February 2016

[4] de Beauvoir, Simone, *The Second Sex*, op. cit.

[5] Julian, Kate, 'Why Are Young People Having So Little Sex?', *The Atlantic*, December 2018, https://www.theatlantic.com/magazine/archive/2018/12/the-sex-recession/573949/

[6] Gibran, Kahlil, *The Prophet* (Vintage Classics, 2014)

[7] Pindar, *The Olympian and Pythian Odes* (Franklin Classics Trade Press, 2018)

[8] Brown, Brené, *The Power of Vulnerability*, TED Talk, 2010, https://www.ted.com/talks/brene_brown_on_vulnerability?language=en

[9] Murdoch, Iris, *Existentialists and Mystics: Writings on Philosophy and Literature* (Penguin New Edition, 1999)

CHAPTER 6: BEING AT WORK

[1] 'More UK workers are skipping lunch – and paying the price, Total Jobs survey, 11 September 2017, https://www.totaljobs.com/insidejob/price-lunch-breaks-research/

[2] Homer, *The Odyssey* (Penguin Classics, 2003)

[3] Weaver, Libby, *Rushing Woman's Syndrome* (Hay House UK, 1997)

[4] Bluedorn, Allen C.; Turban, Daniel B. and Love, Mary Sue, 'The Effects of Stand-Up and Sit-Down Meeting Formats on Meeting Outcomes', *Journal of Applied Pyschology*, 1994, Vol. 84, No. 2, pp. 277–285

[5] Anon, *The English Gentlewoman: A Practical Manual for Young Ladies on Their Entry into Society*, ibid.

[6] de Beauvoir, Simone, *The Second Sex*

[7] http://changingminds.org/explanations/power/soft_power.htm

[8] Angelou, Maya, Facebook post, 9 June 2013

CHAPTER 7: BEING IN CLOTHES

[1] Day, Elizabeth, *How to Fail* (Fourth Estate, 2019); *How to Fail with Elizabeth Day*, https://howtofail.podbean.com

[2] Wilde, Oscar, *The Picture of Dorian Gray* (Wordsworth Classics, 1992)

[3] Apfel, Iris, *Accidental Icon* (Harper Design, 2018)

[4] *The English Gentlewoman*, op. cit.

[5] Maslow, A. H., 'A Theory of Human Motivation', *Psychological Review*, 50(4), 370–96, http://dx.doi.org/10.1037/h0054346

[6] 'The Benefits of Retail Therapy: Making Purchase Decisions Reduces Residual Sadness', *Journal of Consumer Psychology*, July 2014, https://www.researchgate.net/publication/259520781_The_Benefits_of_Retail_Therapy_Making_Purchase_Decisions_Reduces_Residual_Sadness

[7] Beckett, Samuel, *Happy Days*, in *The Complete Works of Samuel Beckett* (Faber & Faber, New Edition, 1998)

CHAPTER 8: BEING A FAMILY

[1] Brave for You', The xx

[2] Kierkegaard, Søren, *Journals* IV. A. 164 (1843)

[3] Woolf, Virginia, *The Waves*, ibid.

[4] *Paris is Burning*, directed by Jennie Livingston, 2010

[5] Beresiner, Sophie, 'The Mother Project', *The Times*

[6] de Beauvoir, Simone, *All Men Are Mortal* (Virago Modern Classics, 1995)

[7] YouGov survey, 'What Will British Families be Arguing About This Christmas?', 18 December 2018, https://yougov.co.uk/topics/lifestyle/articles-reports/2018/12/18/what-will-british-families-be-arguing-about-christ

CHAPTER 9: BEING ONLINE
[1] *You've Got Mail*, written and directed by Nora Ephron, 1998
[2] Ephron, Nora, 'The Six Stages of E-Mail', *The New York Times*, 1 July 2007, https://www.nytimes.com/2007/07/01/opinion/01ephron.html
[3] Brown, Tina, *The Vanity Fair Diaries: 1983–92* (Weidenfeld & Nicolson, 2017)
[4] Stevenson, Robert Louis, *The Strange Case of Dr Jekyll and Mr Hyde and Other Tales of Terror* (Penguin Classics, 2003)
[5] Sontag, Susan, *On Photography* (Penguin, 1979)
[6] https://edition.cnn.com/2018/10/03/health/selfie-deaths-trnd/index.html
[7] Plato, *The Allegory of the Cave* (Penguin Classics, 3rd edition, 2007)

INDEX

Page numbers in **bold** refer to recipes; *n* refers to footnotes

ACKNOWLEDGEMENTS

My wife Jenny's kindness, patience and optimism encouraged me to begin this process of building a good and happy life and I'm lucky to share it with her.

Our daughter Ettie was born the month before I started writing this, and the book, and I, have grown with her.

Thank you to my mum Jenny and my dad Roger for their constant love and support. Also to Aunty Cheryl, my cousin Romy and the Southan family. I am grateful to be surrounded by so many gentlemen as well. One of my best friends, Will Simpson, has been recovering from major surgery to remove cancer as I have been writing these chapters and I have taken much inspiration from his strength and positivity.

Thank you to Marie Maurer and Hannah Swerling for reading drafts and giving me smart notes and to Joe Marriott for motivating me always.

It is fitting that I have worked closest with two absolute gentlewomen, my literary agent Abigail Bergstrom and editor Romilly Morgan. Thank you.

I appreciate the work done on this book by everyone at Octopus Publishing and am hugely grateful to all the women (and the drag queen) who gave their time and ideas to me as interviewees – I'm honoured to share their voices in my story.

Thank you to all the journalists, writers, poets and philosophers whose words I have quoted throughout. These texts have shaped me in so many ways.

LOTTE JEFFS

In 2016 Lotte Jeffs won 'Writer of The Year' at the Press and Publishing Association Awards. The following year she was shortlisted for 'Columnist of the Year' for her *ELLE* magazine column, Lotte's Lexicon. She has been a features writer and columnist for the past 15 years, writing for the *Guardian*, the *Saturday Times*, the *Sunday Times*, the *Evening Standard*, *YOU Magazine* and *ELLE*. Lotte has enjoyed a successful career on staff at magazines most recently as Deputy Editor and Acting Editor in Chief of *ELLE*. She has appeared on TV and radio and regularly hosts and participates in industry panel discussions.

Lotte was head-hunted by the global advertising agency Ogilvy to join its UK office as a Creative Director. She now works freelance as a writer and creative consultant. Having pivoted into a different, but similar, industry she continues to keep a toe in journalism, writing a Notebook column for the *Evening Standard*, features for the national press and celebrity cover interviews for newspaper supplements and magazines.

She lives in London with her wife, Jenny, and their daughter.